Empath to Mystic

The Art of Mastering Your Intuition and Fearlessly Being Yourself

Aaran Solh

This book is dedicated to my daughter Soffeah, for helping me remember what happiness, innocence, and wisdom are, and what it truly means to be a child of Earth. May the benefit this book brings help create a safer world for all the children of Earth (yourself, dear reader, included).

Contents

GETTING STARTED

Thank you for reading Empath to Mystic!

Before getting started, I'd like to invite you to visit my website where you you can join the Inner Circle and download free supplemental material such as guided meditations, videos, and journaling worksheets.

www.AaranSolh.com

Finally, as an author, I highly appreciate the feedback I get from my readers. If you enjoy this book you are about to read, please consider leaving a short review on Amazon.com. It will help others make an informed decision before buying my book.

With deep gratitude,

Aaran Solh

Foreword

In a world filled with digital, physical, and inner noise, it is challenging to navigate from a centered and present place. And this challenge is magnified if you are sensitive to other people's thoughts, energy, and/or emotions. So many people now struggle to stay open-hearted and present because they are overwhelmed with so much information and so many feelings. I'm always looking for good books to help people who are energetically sensitive, or have shut down their intuition due to fear or trauma. Aaran's Empath to Mystic book is a beautiful, step-by-step guide for anyone wanting to ground into their gifts of intuition and knowing.

I first met Aaran through his partner, now wife, Aryana. I've known her since she was 13, when we both apprenticed with don Miguel Ruiz, author of The Four Agreements. After not seeing Aryana for many years I was delighted when she moved to my town and introduced me to her beloved, Aaran. We spent many nights having long conversations and I was always impressed by his passion, clarity, and gentle heart.

When Aaran and Aryana announced they were leaving Austin to live in Southeast Asia I was both excited for how they would grow and deepen their message. I was so delighted to read Aaran's Empath to Mystic, which shares the many lessons and skills he has cultivated throughout his lifetime. This is a much needed, important book.

It is one thing to realize that you are sensitive, or an empath. It is another to get a loving guide for how to use your super powers to grow your consciousness and love instead of getting swamped or always feeling drained and exhausted.

Empath to Mystic offers so much, in a clear, concise way. Aaran's four pillars of intuition will help you rebuild your foundation from the bottom up. Whether you have shut down your inner voice, or you are overwhelmed with how much data you are always receiving, you will find a friend and teacher in these pages. Each chapter includes not only valuable information and guidance, but also specific visualizations and meditations, doable action steps, and inquiry questions to deepen your understanding.

If you are ready to reclaim your inner voice and begin to be guided by your own knowing, you are in good hands with Aaran. May you shed the layers of confusion, hurt, and fears to allow the light of your radiant, peaceful, purpose to shine forth and be a guide to yourself and others.

–HeatherAsh Amara,
author of Warrior Goddess Training and
Awaken Your Inner Fire

FINDING MY POWER ON THE JOURNEY FROM EMPATH TO MYSTIC

mys·tic

A person who has a spiritual apprehension of truths that are beyond the intellect and who allows those truths to guide their actions.

When I was a child, I could sense what others around me were feeling and thinking. As I grew up, as so many empaths and spiritually attuned children experience, I was gravely misunderstood. I did not fit in very well to school structures and felt awkward socially. I was constantly in trouble and always being picked on as the 'odd one out.' As most empaths who grew up unrecognized and unsupported do, I shut down and 'checked out' - functioning in the physical world but never truly feeling my emotions or experiencing life fully. As so many sensitive children end up these days, I became numb, anxious, and depressed.

As a teenager, I found other kids to surround myself with who also didn't fit in. We wanted to be left alone to drink and smoke away the pain and were constantly chastised and punished by parents, teachers, police, and court systems alike. But I was fortunate - as a teen, something out of the ordinary happened to me. I was exposed to mysticism and spirituality by people who weren't trying to save me, change me, or use me. I was fortunate to find adult mentors who respected me for who I was, took me seriously, and treated me with respect. They saved me from a life of pain, shame, and fear.

My soul had taken refuge in the spirit world because living consciously on Earth had been too painful. One of my mentors even described me as having feet firmly planted on the earth, head in the sky, and nothing connecting the two! Many spiritual seekers, empaths and sensitive people end up living this way. They fully function, taking care of others, going to and from work, but inside they feel anxious, depressed, or numb. They are aware of the energies and emotions around them but feel depleted by that ability, not knowing how to harness their strength or communicate to others what they see and feel.

They may allow their natural ability to love and have compassion to be used by people who take advantage of them. It is an incredibly difficult way to live.

It took some time, but I learned to embrace my abilities as an empath on a journey of spiritual awakening. Over many years of studying with spiritual teachers, shamans, and mystics around the world I learned to process my emotions and to process my knowledge of the emotions of other people around me in a grounded, stable, loving, and connected way. I learned to allow the physical world to connect with the intuitive, spiritual, and mystical one and invited them all to make a home together in my body. I learned to have boundaries and direct my skill intentionally so that it doesn't randomly fluctuate. Because of that, I have been able to help hundreds of people as a grounded intuitive with solid energetic boundaries. Not only without getting overwhelmed, but being very happy and joyful in my service, and always with the feeling that there is meaning to my life.

In my desire to help others walk the same path, the time finally came for me to create systems to help empaths, sensitive people, and people who are awakening to their spiritual nature do what I did. But I wanted them to be able to transform their lives and evolve their capacity for feeling peace, freedom, and connection in the comfort of their own home. To that end, the system I present in this book focuses on building your intuition, because that is the greatest gift of an empath and it is the best way to learn to connect to the higher wisdom within you. You can turn your gift of sensitivity inward instead of constantly outward. You can clear the emotional and mental channels, allow your inner voice to shine, and your authentic spiritual gifts to be unveiled, both to yourself and to the world.

You can live as the spiritual guide and artist you came into this world to be, even though, unlike the villages, clans, or native cultures of old, there may not be a recognized role for you. In old-world villages and native tribes you would have been recognized and appreciated for your gifts. You would have been sent to apprentice with the village shaman or artist guild, or been honored with a room at the local monastery - celebrated instead of made to feel like an outsider.

Today we have to be stronger. We have to come together as a community and recognize our strengths. We must lift each other up and remember that we are the bridges, here to guide people to goodness and wholeness in appreciation of each other and of nature. We mustn't give up on humanity! We have the power to be their artists, shamans, peacemakers, and prophets. To be the inspired visionaries who together can create a movement that ends the isolation, depression, and destruction in which so many people live. We are the ones, there are no others.

There are two paths for you to choose from. One leads you forward into the unknown - into healing, connection, awareness and yes, the challenge of being big, being creative, and being seen for who you are. The other path leads to more of the same - to the challenge of struggling to fit in and keeping yourself small, confused, and possibly in pain. This book and the community behind it can lead you down the first path - to finding your life purpose, to remembering why you incarnated, to being strong in the face of oppression and adversity, and to not accepting life as 'the way it is' anymore.

Mastering your intuition will lead you to a balanced harnessing of your mystical power and give you a grounded, meaningful, and creative life. It will be challenging, but it will be the good kind of challenging. The kind that makes you feel alive. The kind that makes you feel inspired even though you have no idea what is around the next bend in the road or how you are going to accomplish your vision; or how, indeed, you are going to find a vision to pursue!

Opening to your inner voice, and letting it heal and guide you gives you a new best friend. A friend that is, "nearer to you than yourself," as the poem by Rumi quoted in the first chapter of this book tells us. When you open to your inner voice and reconnect your spiritual self to your earth-bound self, that is what happens. "The friend comes into the body," as another line by Rumi tells us. Come along for the ride, learn to trust your inner voice, and let it lead you on the adventure of a lifetime. *Your* lifetime!

CHOOSING YOUR INNER VOICE AS NAVIGATOR

When you look for God,
God is in the look of your eyes
In the thought of looking
Nearer to you than yourself
~Rumi

THE JOURNEY OF BECOMING YOU

On your journey of self-discovery there have no doubt been moments where you have glimpsed what it's like to be completely free. Able to follow your inner voice and intuition clearly and consistently. Moments where you have been full of energy and passion, able to face whatever challenges stood in your way.

But the glimpses are probably erratic, and maybe you are unable to grab hold of them. You might find yourself dipping into sadness and longing to give your gifts to the world, yet still not having a grasp of what they are. Your personal struggles or inability to trust in your own decisions may create a tiredness that doesn't seem to fade with positive thinking. You may find yourself buckling under the weight of perceived limitations instead of living every moment from the creative energy pulsing inside you.

Maybe you feel like Denise.

She wrote me this:

"Hi Aaran,

It is no coincidence that I am here and found you...There is a longing in my heart/soul to free myself of the stuck life I find myself in and live the life I was meant to live! I truly believe there is an amazing life for me... filled with a sense of purpose, peace, exploration and abundance. My fear and lack of belief in myself holds me back. Daily, I am making strides to change these limiting beliefs and am trying to create new habits... Soooo hard!"

Maybe, like Denise, you realize that there is a way to stay connected to the wisdom within you at all times. And maybe, like her, you are not sure how to anchor what you know in a way that actually changes your patterns of thought and behavior. If you are reading this, however, you must still have hope for a sense of true connection. Hope that you can embrace change in your body, your personality, and your very identity. Hope that you can discover how to follow your insights and intuitions - your *inner voice* - at all times.

In order to follow your inner voice at all times you have to master two things:

1. Distinguishing your inner voice from other voices
2. Finding the courage to follow it

These are two separate problems. First, you have to get beyond the head chatter and the many voices of other people in your head to find your own inner voice. Once you have done that, you have to learn to trust it, feel worthy of it, and courageously push past the fear that comes up when your inner voice guides you into the unknown. In this book you will find the information, practices and action steps you need to help you master these challenges. Most importantly, you will discover the four pillars of intuition, and when you build them, you will create a home for your inner voice to dwell in the temple of your body.

THE FOUR PILLARS OF INTUITION

The pillars of intuition are four conditions that must be met in your psyche to be able to hear and follow your inner voice - the voice that is speaking to you when you say you had an *intuition*. The *inner voice* is the voice of love and higher intelligence that lives inside of you. The *intuition* is the conscious perception of that voice. It is the gap between the inner voice and the intuition appearing in your conscious mind that this book will help you bridge, allowing you to truly be yourself.

By understanding the four pillars, their challenges, and building blocks, you can enable your inner voice to consciously, regularly, and predictably provide answers to all your questions. Mastering the four pillars helps you clear the channels of communication and gives you the courage to listen to what comes through.

The Four Pillars: Vision, Connection, Receptivity and Creativity

When building the pillar of vision, you uncover your core motivations. You create a vision for yourself that serves as a faraway beacon to aspire to as you sail the dark seas of this world. You gain a sense of purpose by discovering your own highest potential and path of service in the world. Without a sense of purpose and a vision of your highest potential, you won't have enough strength to face the challenges on your path. You will find that you lack the discipline to press on and disempowering thoughts will kill your ambitions. When building your pillar of vision, the main challenge is overcoming a lack of motivation and a fear of failure.

When building the pillar of connection, you discover your relationship to a source of spiritual nourishment and love within you; a source that provides a lifeline when your mind is drowning in other people's voices. Without this connection, you will continue to seek nourishment, love and validation only from external sources. If you don't balance your internal knowing with your need for external love, you will never have the courage to make bold choices in your life and face possible rejection when you do. When building the pillar of connection, the main challenge is finding and amplifying your own voice among the many voices in your head and overcoming the fear of isolation.

When building the pillar of receptivity, you develop a consistent ability to trust in and receive support from a spiritual source within and from people who walk the path with you. Without support you will quickly lose steam and perpetuate a feeling of abandonment and lack of self-worth within yourself. You will continue to chase your tail, caught in a vortex of boredom and feeling overwhelmed, never managing to find the time for what really matters in life. When building the pillar of receptivity, the main challenge is learning to trust yourself and overcoming the fear of being out of control.

When building the pillar of creativity, you weave your vision into reality by connecting to a deep place of silence in your heart. The kind of silence that is born when you allow yourself to fully experience your life with all its joys and pains. To unleash your creative juices, your insights need to flow freely, but bottled up emotions can create a swampy numbness in your heart that your insights can't flow through. This swamp creates circuitous head chatter that makes it impossible to make positive choices for yourself. The main challenge in building the pillar of creativity is facing the pain in your own heart and in the world and overcoming the fear of exposure.

The four pillars of intuition are in constant flux and are built up or broken down to varying degrees at different times in your life. The more you actively learn to build the pillars and maintain them, the more stable they become and the easier it becomes for your inner voice to communicate with you and successfully guide you. Practices for this are given throughout the book and in special chapters dedicated to the topic.

Being able to hear your inner voice at every fork in the road is crucial to making the right decisions in your life. The decisions that will bring you what you want. Some people think there's a magical 'secret' to creating the life you want. But creating the life you want is not magic. It's a process of regularly making the right decisions to get yourself there. And it's the process of bringing your inner voice *into* your body.

It is your birthright to fully embody the spiritual insights you have gained and to be the best version of yourself. Following your intuition is how you do that. By allowing it in past your unconscious fear and conditioning. Past your perceived limitations, lack of motivation, and lack of belief and trust. Past the head chatter and past all those voices of other people who have told you what to do.

HOW DO YOU REBUILD YOUR PILLARS?

Whether or not you are aware of it, you have a memory of what it is like to have your four pillars and your connection to your inner voice fully established. Everybody has this memory because we were each born into a body that was fully connected to its source. Your memory of it might not be verbal or visual but it is deep inside you and that is why you yearn for it. If you had never had it, you would never think to search for it.

Somewhere deep inside, you know what it's like to be fully connected to your intuition and inner voice, to have solid boundaries and inner strength. Take a moment to feel the truth of that - close your eyes right now, take a deep breath, and feel... As you grow up, however, you become, as Western psychology puts it, *conditioned* (or *domesticated* as the Toltecs say). You lose your freedom and you lose your innate ability to follow your inner voice. Your four pillars are beaten down and they end up looking like a deserted Roman ruin.

When you enter this world, you come in as a helpless infant. Almost immediately the adults in your life try to manipulate your behavior using reward and punishment. You are punished - made to feel pain and fear over and over again as the adults in your life try to control you. This is true no matter how kind or loving your parents were but it is especially true if you grew up in a violent environment.

Reward is no better. As children we were all taught to be trained monkeys. To eat our carrots to get dessert. To finish our homework so we can play and we were taught to be respectful in order to get love. For most people, growing up was a series of if-then conditions. If I do this... I get punished or I get rewarded. For most people, that journey never ended - they still look outside themselves for validation. This is why it is so hard to turn inward to your own intuition.

Your task as an adult on a path of reclaiming your innocence and inner voice is to de-condition yourself in order to become peaceful and free again. To un-learn the habit of choosing to behave a certain way out of a desire to be rewarded or the fear of punishment. Your goal is to see everything through the eyes of the miracle that is the very existence of life. To see the world with the innocence of a child, the capable body and intelligence of an adult, and inspired by the wisdom of your inner voice.

It's pretty straight forward but it's not easy. Instead of unconscious conditions telling you what to do, you want your inner voice to be your navigator. Your inner voice sees so much further than your conditioned mind is capable of seeing. And because of that, Its messages may seem illogical and even dangerous to follow. As a defense, your unconscious mind turns on the head chatter, leading to doubt and confusion, all in the name of keeping you safe. The result is that before you ever get a chance to know what your intuition is saying, your unconscious fear blocks it from even reaching you.

The purpose of this book is to give you the knowledge and tools you need to help you decondition yourself from old patterns and to help you master new conditions that create a home for your inner voice in your body and your conscious mind. New conditions that will ultimately enable you to perceive your inner voice in the form of intuitions and free it to sculpt your life in the ways you pray for and to serve the highest good.

Building the four pillars is the process of re-awakening to the fundamental truth that you *are* your inner voice. It's not a short road and it's not an easy one, but the alternative is to stay stuck. And no matter how safe or comfortable your life may be at the moment, feeling like you are betraying something at your core is not a feeling you want to carry with you to your grave.

THE PATH OF MASTERY

A LESSON IN GARDENING

They say it is more important to give a hungry person a gardening lesson than to give them a cucumber. In that spirit, this is not merely a theoretical book. It is interactive! Building mastery in anything is not an easy process. So first of all, congratulations on making this choice for yourself. Congratulations on joining the multitudes of people who are waking up to who they really are and transforming the world for the better. Congratulations on finally letting go of the comfortable and the familiar and taking a leap into the unknown!

In this book you will learn how to experience your inner voice and have it guide you. You will learn how to utilize that connection to release your old, unconscious, self-sabotaging beliefs. You will learn how to accelerate your growth through receptivity and an internal connection to a source of love and nourishment. Finally, you will learn how to allow that love to flow through you, so that your heart can once again create from a place of childlike innocence and love.

The practices in this book will lead you to connect to your inner voice in a clear and consistent way, but you have to do them for the changes to take root. To make real change in your life you need to create new ways of thinking and you need to make the unconscious conscious. You also need to give your body a new experience of life as a vessel for your higher consciousness. In this book there are three ways for you to do that:

1. **The first is obvious - read the book:** The information itself is valuable. It will give you new things to think about and offer fresh perspectives on your ability to grow as a spiritual being.

2. **Journaling prompts:** There are pauses throughout this book where you are invited to think about the material and write about how it applies to you personally. These steps allow you to make your unconscious thoughts, conscious, bringing about real transformation. In order to fully utilize this feature, you'll want to get a journal to write your answers in. You can also visit the author's website where you can download a PDF with all the journaling prompts and use it as your journal: www.AaranSolh.com.

3. **Action steps, which are divided into two:**
   A. **Practices and visualizations:** You can do these while you are reading the book. They will usually only take a few minutes to contemplate, visualize or feel.
   B. **Action steps to take in your life:** Without taking new action steps, nothing will change. Taking action sends a clear message to your inner voice that you are ready to be present in that relationship, and that you are committed to making real change in your life and the world.

When you reach inquiry questions, invitations to stop and feel or meditate on a topic, don't continue reading, stop and do the practice. Stop and *feel*. Having a non-verbal, feeling experience is what changes your unconscious mind. If you want real change, please treat this as you would any other class, by practicing and doing your work! If you find yourself stuck on a specific prompt or action step, however, don't stay stuck for long. It's much better to continue reading the book and then circle back around to the action item later. You don't want to allow your inability to follow through in the moment to become an excuse to stop entirely or an obstacle to progressing to other practices.

UNJUST PAIN

Becoming a person who follows their inner voice not only helps you fulfill your own life purpose. It also helps you fulfill our collective goal as human beings of living in safe, peaceful, and balanced relationships with each other and the planet. There is a lot of pain in the world caused by natural disasters, uncertainty, and disease. To create complete safety and peace in our external world may be an impossibility but we can strive to create a world where we have peace with each other and there is no need for us to inflict pain on each other or compete to survive.

This can only be accomplished by each of us doing our own inner work to clear ourselves of our conditioning, connecting to our inner voice, and being willing to embrace its guidance. When we do that work, we create harmony within ourselves that can radiate outward. We fly like a flock of birds, swerving together as the flock changes direction, because the inner voice that speaks through you, is the same inner voice that speaks through me. Because we ultimately emanate from the same source, and when we are conscious of that, we live in peace.

Take a moment to truly feel that - the ability to live in harmony and peace. Take a few deep breaths, relax, close your eyes and tune into your body. Then ask yourself, 'What would it feel like in my body to be at peace?'

Go ahead, take a moment to stop and do this practice.

If this was challenging for you in any way, that's natural, because you didn't grow up in peace. You grew up having to compete and being frightened of consequences, worried that if you didn't do the right thing, you would be abandoned or punished. Maybe when you close your eyes and imagine what peace feels like in your body an unconscious fear kicks in - fear that tells you you should be something other than who you are. The fear that if you loosen control you will do the 'wrong thing,' and somebody will inflict pain on you. Just like the unjust pain that was inflicted on you as a child. And it is important to remember that no matter how justified the people in your life felt about causing you that pain, it was still unjustified.

Journaling prompt:
Who would you be if no one had ever inflicted pain on you?

This was my response:
"I would be a person surrounded by joy and beauty. One who takes things slow and who appreciates nature. I would be a person who could sit like a child and stare at a running brook for hours, enjoying the peace of the forest. I would have a definitive knowing that I deserve to be loved, cared for, and tended to like a precious jewel." ~Aaran Solh

I never would have known that about myself if I hadn't written down the answer. More importantly, I never would have *felt it* and so I wouldn't be one step closer to being that person.

To connect to your answer to this question, first, close your eyes and feel the answer in your heart. Just feel. Experience the person within you who never had to experience purposeful pain inflicted on them by others. Then ask yourself, 'Who would I be if no one had ever inflicted pain on me?' Write down what comes to you.

FINGERS AND BRAINS

This book will help you think about things, and it will give you the opportunities you need to stop and practice what you just learned, as it is only through practice, implementation, and repetition that you can change. That you can re-integrate your long lost inner voice and put it back at the head of the table. And the best part? When you follow the guidance of your inner voice (the guidance that comes to you as intuitions), you create a ripple effect that gives permission and teaches others to do the same.

But what happens when you don't follow your intuition? Think about it like this: What would go through your mind if you tried to bend your fingers but they wouldn't bend? Meaning, if you went to pick up your keys and your arm moved but when you got to the keys, your fingers just did nothing no matter how much you wanted them to? You would probably think you were in serious trouble - that maybe you were having a stroke or maybe you had some kind of nerve damage.

Think of the relationship between your fingers and your brain as the same as the relationship between yourself and your inner voice. The fingers are different from your hand. And they are different from your arm and they are different from your brain. But they are not *separate* from them. You are the fingers. When the inner voice bends you or moves you and you don't move, it means there's something wrong. It's a symptom of an underlying systemic malfunction. It is a shattering, a breakage, and what is required is healing and cleansing. A re-integrating of that banished inner voice.

You are different from your inner voice but you are not separate. When in a healthy state, you and your inner voice are aligned. You are like your brain and the parts of the body it moves. And before your ego jumps in and complains about being controlled by an external force, realize that the inner voice is not an external force. It is very much a part of you but you have secluded it and exiled it. You have set it aside in favor of creating a 'you' that better suits the needs and conditions that other people and society at large have imposed. It may *seem* external, but it is not.

Your intuitions are like the messages sent from your brain to your fingers. They are the wisdom of your inner voice arriving in your conscious and verbal mind through a maze of thoughts and conditionings. In this book, you will be clearing that pathway between your inner voice and conscious mind so that those messages are no longer blocked by fear and bottled up emotion. At the end, you will recognize that you *are* your inner voice and there will be no more argument about who gets to move the finger. No more paralysis.

The journey of re-integrating your inner voice is the journey of becoming whole once again. It is the journey where after going around and around in circles to find yourself, you can finally take a moment to breathe and then something clicks. It is the story of The Alchemist. It is The Never Ending Story. It is The Wizard of Oz. It is the journey that you have to go on in order to finally realize that what you are looking for is at home, where you left it and it has always been available to you. "Nearer to you than yourself," as Rumi's quote at the beginning of this book tells us.

By the end of this book, you will recognize that you have a genius that is unique to you. A genius that is the way that the inner voice shines through your unique prism of body and mind. No matter how that genius manifests itself, when you bring it to light, it will give you a feeling of purpose and strength. And you will start to experience that purpose and strength by first building your pillar of vision.

Take action:

Wiggle your fingers. Then close your eyes, take a few deep breaths and imagine being a finger wiggled by your inner voice, with no resistance whatsoever. After a minute of this visualization, think of a situation in your life where you feel stuck and then imagine your inner voice moving you (as the finger) in the direction it wants you to go. What was your experience? What insights into the situation did you have? Write them down in your journal.

WORKING WITH A GROUP

To support you further in making real change, you can work through Empath to Mystic with other people you know who also want to grow their connection with their inner voice. Being held accountable to a group will give you the extra strength and motivation you need to complete the book and see real change awaken within.

Another benefit of working in a group is that there is enormous power in simply being witnessed in your process, your struggles, and your striving for authenticity and truth. Your friends can also do *that* for you. And you know what? They don't even have to live on the same continent as you to support you. They can be anywhere in the world!

If you believe that having a group to support you in developing mastery over your intuition would be beneficial to you then take action. Take a moment to think of four people who you think might do this work with you and list them in your journal. If you can't think of four people, go through your list of Facebook friends to refresh your memory of the people you know.

Once you have four names, use the momentum to take further action by reaching out to them and asking them to join you. Do it not only for yourself, but also because this book may truly help them. Go ahead and do it now.

Did you complete the journaling prompts and practices in the introductory chapters?

YES - I'm going to build my pillar of vision now.

NO - I will go back and do them right now before I continue so that I start my journey from empath to mystic off on the right foot.

BUILDING THE PILLAR OF VISION

THE PILLAR

Your vision is the fire that fuels your motivation and determination. The kind of motivation that allows you to pick yourself up every time you falter and fall. The kind of determination that wakes you up early in the morning to do your practice or pursue your craft.

Having a clear vision of what is possible, not just for yourself but also for the world, allows you to overcome your internal voices of doubt because when those internal doubts start bombarding you (and they will), it can feel like you are facing an impenetrable fortress. The doubts, standing there, taunting you from their lofty battlements trying to persuade you that it might be better to keep your head down and not take back your rightful throne.

Your vision is the artillery that gets you into the gate. Your vision is what makes you charge the walls despite feeling weak and afraid, knowing in your heart of hearts that, no matter how real they seem, the walls are only thoughts in your mind. Knowing that as you approach those walls they will turn to mist, which you will scatter by shining the clear light of your inner voice.

Without vision, you will ignore the calling of your inner voice to push past fear and take a leap into the unknown. You will hide in the comfort of the familiar even though you crave a more fulfilling life. Your vision is like the rockets that allow the space shuttle to overcome gravity and fly into space. And when you think about it, space is a hostile environment. You have to have a really good reason to go up there; to willingly leave the green and blue of Earth and go off into the unknown without knowing the exact dangers you might be facing.

Powerful visionaries include people like Dr. Martin Luther King Jr., America's civil rights hero and Annie Kenney, a leading figure in England's woman's suffrage movement. But in your daily life, they are also the people down the street who spend their days tinkering in the garage, inventing new things. The visionary is also your friend who has shown up again and again to teach their workshop even though only a few people show up every time. They do it because they believe in it, and they know success is a process, not because anybody has guaranteed them an outcome.

You need to find the power to act. But without a vision, your inner voice doesn't know in which direction to point you and the gravitational pull of the familiar makes you doubt yourself into inaction. So if you are in a place where your comfort is more important to you than your curiosity and fulfillment, your rockets won't have the power to lift you out of the atmosphere. If your fear is stronger than your desire to explore, you will never charge the walls of the castle. The tables need to be turned!

You need to make your fear of living the same day over and over again for the rest of your life more powerful than gravity (the inertia and fear that keep you stuck where you are). More powerful than the desire for the safety of the familiar. More powerful than your disbelief that something better *is* waiting for you. And, critically, more powerful than your fear of surrendering to the unknown. Building your pillar of vision means you are willing to sacrifice the comfort of the familiar and break new ground with real world actions that have the potential to make the world a better place, even though no one can guarantee the results.

THE CHALLENGE: PUSHING A BOULDER UP A HILL

If you haven't built a vision of what's possible for yourself, then there's nothing driving you or pulling you forward. You might find yourself sitting around wishing for a more fulfilling life but not knowing how to attain it. It could be because you don't even know what 'it' is! If you haven't defined it, you can't take clear steps towards it.

It is also possible that the modern era of convenience has taken over your life and that you don't have much room to create excitement and adventure for yourself. In the modern day (for the most part), you have what you need at your fingertips, and generally speaking, nothing is endangering your life on a regular basis, so there is no deep-seated motivation to take risks.

If you are still building your pillar of vision, then all too often you might choose to rest comfortably by the fire, drinking a glass of wine or watching television, unmotivated and undisciplined in your pursuit of your connection to your inner voice and intuition. In that place of boredom and lack of motivation, you may even turn to substances because substances mimic the cathartic feelings of contentment, confidence, and relaxation normally created by the mystical connection you have with the universe.

If not substances, you might try and get excitement from a physical workout, gambling, food, sex, or anything else pleasurable. This may work for a while but none of these substitutes can give you real, long-lasting pleasure and a sense of meaning and purpose. The kind of purpose that comes from sticking your neck out there with a personal vision for yourself and taking a stand for something you really believe in. Even if you fail repeatedly while pursuing it.

The irony is that without a degree of struggle or real need in your life, the desperation to make your self-inquiry, education or work in the world a priority may not be there. And even though your intelligence pushes you to go beyond that kind of numb comfort, without a clear vision, it can sometimes feel like you are pushing an impossibly large boulder up a hill. If there is no fire at the bottom of the hill, your motivation for getting to the top with that boulder isn't as strong as it could be.

Journaling prompt:

Write down at least 3 things you want for yourself or changes you want to see in your life. These could be things you want to accomplish or do, relationships you want to build, things that make you happy, skills you want to learn, simply being, or anything else that makes you feel alive and are motivated by. In addition, write down at least 3 changes you would like to see happen in the world (whether or not you believe you can help make those changes happen).

Below each item write an action step that you can take in that direction. If you can't think of anything specific, your action step could be to research what you can do or to meditate on it. Below each action item, put down the time frame in which you are going to take this action.

Note: Don't allow worrying about success or failure in the long term stop you from doing this exercise. Make your desires big, but make your action steps small enough to be completely attainable.

It should look like this:

Things I want for myself:

1)

Action step:

Time frame:

2)

Action step:

Time frame:

3)

Action step:

Time frame:

Changes I want to see in the world:

1)

Action step:

Time frame:
2)
Action step:
Time frame:
3)
Action step:
Time frame:

Journaling prompt:

Think about times in your life where your vision of the best possible outcome wasn't strong enough to see you through to success. A project, a class, a relationship… anything. These could be times when you just didn't believe achieving something greater was possible. Or times when you gave up on your vision, convinced there was no way you could achieve it. Write about these times in your life.

A VISION IS SIMPLE

Creating a vision for yourself and the world is about taking back the reins of your life from external circumstances and your conditioning and giving it an authentic direction to go in. Developing a vision and becoming a master of your own destiny is simple. A vision is merely the imagining of the best possible outcome for yourself and the world. The best possible outcome that you can imagine *right now,* be it for your work, finances, love life, the environment, or for knowing and living your very purpose in this world.

Once you establish that vision for yourself, then the fulfillment of your vision is a process of adhering to the guidance of your intuition as you walk the path. It is also the process of allowing new information to flow in so that you don't stay fixed on your desired outcome. A vision is something that evolves over time, not something you stay attached to. It changes with each step that you take. It is as alive as you, and it is living in the *right now* where things are always taking shape to make your vision for the best possible outcome, well… even better.

Are you familiar with the famous speech by Dr. Martin Luther King Jr., 'I Have A Dream?' Did you know he had prepared an entirely different speech for that day? He started giving it and then received a clear message from his inner voice to set it aside. He trusted and allowed his vision to evolve in the moment, and because he listened, he was able to inspire millions of people and social justice movements around the world.

To really be successful in this world, your choices need to be based on a clear connection with your inner voice and intuition. Without a strong vision for yourself, you may be content to curl up on your comfortable couch and ignore the world rather than fight for something better. You might spend your life living in what Buddhist philosophy refers to as, *the realm of the gods,* where all-mighty and immortal beings live, who lack for nothing and can do anything. Beings who don't suffer from pain, loss, and discontentment.

The realm of the gods is a metaphor for how you might find yourself living on Earth. For example, when you have social or financial privilege that removes the need to struggle for your survival and freedom or even when you lack resources but are afraid of risking what you have or going outside of the familiar - choosing your comfort zone over the unknown. Creating a powerful vision for yourself is your way out of this realm of the gods / comfort-zone trap.

When there is no pain and no lack, there is no fire burning at the bottom of the hill urging you to push that boulder onward. That is why being in touch with your personal experience of pain, loss, and discontentment is crucial to creating your vision, and especially crucial for *accomplishing* your vision. Staying in touch with the feeling of what you never again want to happen to you or to others, fuels your fire like nothing else. It drives you to be of service in the best possible way.

When you take stock of the pain and loss you have suffered in your life, you will notice that alongside that pain there is a desire that no one else ever experience that same pain. It is a natural and organic human compassionate instinct, and as a first step to creating your vision, you can utilize it. It doesn't even matter if you carry a feeling of helplessness when thinking about what you can or cannot do about it right now. Because it isn't about knowing what you *can* do, it is about knowing that you *want* to do it, and trusting that the 'what/how to do' part will follow when you build a clear connection with your inner voice.

As you build and strengthen your pillars of intuition, gaining regular access to your inner voice, you will accomplish something even greater. You will allow your vision to be formulated, not only by your own pain, but also by your co-creative positive aspirations. Co-creative with your inner voice and the mystery that lives beyond it. By the end of this book, you will be able to do that, so let that be part of your motivation for getting through it and completing the practices.

Journaling prompts:
1. List at least 5 painful experiences you have had in your life. These can be personal attacks, institutional attitudes, the sorrow you feel over other people's experiences, anything and everything counts if it is painful for you. If you like, list as many painful experiences as you can think of (just the act of making a list can be healing). Later on you will use your answer to help formulate a vision statement.

2. What would you do with your life right now if you had unlimited resources and a limitless supply of cash?

3. What would you set out to accomplish if you knew you couldn't fail - if a successful outcome was one hundred percent guaranteed (no goal is too lofty)?

4. What would you want to do with your life if you knew you only had six months to live?

5. You're on your death bed, and the most important people in your life are around you. What is the greatest wisdom you've gained in your life that you'd want to share?

Take action:

Formulate a vision statement for yourself based on the answers you gave to the questions above. Think about the pain you've experienced in life and how you may feel motivated to work so that nobody else experiences such pain or to help other people heal from the same wounds. Consider the things you would do with unlimited resources and incorporate those. Remember to be in the *right now* with your vision, recognizing that it will evolve over time. Allow yourself to think and dream big, even if you have no idea if you'll ever be able to accomplish this vision in your lifetime. Start the statement with the words, 'I want…' And don't worry about the 'how,' at all - focus only on the, 'I want.'

Journaling prompt:

Can you see the flow of actions and circumstances that would need to happen in order to connect the dot of this moment to the accomplishment of your vision (the one you just wrote)? Keep in mind that the steps you put down here can be very broad and that you don't have to know yet how the middle steps are going to be filled.

For example: Step 1: Create a business plan for my dream business (even though I don't know how to do that yet). Step 2: Find ten million worth of investment for it. Step 3: Hire my first one hundred employees. Step 4: Etc…

You don't need to know *how* the gaps are going to be filled. You just need to know what the steps *are*. So, what are some of the steps you will need to take in order to get from where you are right now, to where your vision is ultimately taking you?

SUICIDE TUESDAY

It is not enough to have a vision. That part is easy. The real struggle is overcoming the *suicide Tuesday* effect and sustaining a fire at the bottom of the hill. A fire that inoculates your vision with a sense of urgency, importance, and meaning. A fire that serves as motivation for you to push that boulder to the top of the hill.

If you are struggling to find discipline and motivation, it probably means that you spend your free time seeking out pleasurable 'escape' style experiences and emotional highs. But the pleasures and the emotional highs that you get from external stimulation (such as watching TV, reading books, playing games, Facebook likes, getting that extra workout in, taking substances, having sex, eating food, or anything else) can make your day-to-day life feel dim in comparison. And that dimness is your number one motivation killer.

As we have already seen, the pleasures of external stimulation can only ever be short-lived. So, if you are taking comfort in the artificial excitements of external stimulation (and we all do, to some degree), there is a price to pay for that. That price is called suicide Tuesday. Suicide Tuesday is a term used in the community of people who take drugs like Ecstasy or LSD regularly. It refers to the sense of pointlessness and depression experienced on Tuesday morning after a weekend of flooding your brain with the neurotransmitters dopamine and serotonin.

Alcohol, other minor substances, living artificial adventures (through TV, games, and books), and other external sources of pleasure, will create the same suicide Tuesday effect - even if to a lesser degree. Getting high on life's pleasures leaves you feeling depressed when your life isn't as thrilling as the moment you got those two hundred Facebook likes, the time you beat your latest high score, when you had the best orgasm of your life, or you went down to the movie theater to watch the latest release. Capitalism as a system depends on this constant running around looking for the next quick fix and entire industries are forced to tap into this addiction mechanism to keep you 'hooked' or they don't survive.

Consider the film industry: Have you noticed how in the past century of filmmaking that movies have gotten faster and faster paced? Take Star Wars for example. The original Star Wars from the 1970's was relatively slow paced. Even the action scenes were slow moving and thoughtful. Now look at the second batch of Star Wars movies to come out and how fast paced they are. The scenes in the second batch of films move from one action rumble to the next without slowing down. You are so high on adrenaline by the end that you can't go another day without doing something else to get the same kind of high, or you experience a suicide Tuesday.

The worst part is that the next time you seek out that high, you will need more of it to get the same effect. This need for more of the same substance to get the same high is called *building up tolerance*. In the world of physical drug addiction, tolerance means that the body needs more and more of a drug in order to get the same effect. But you don't have to look at heroin to understand this. Just look at food, caffeine, and nicotine addiction and you will see how this concept of tolerance has the potential to effect almost everyone.

In the movies, what they do to make sure you keep watching, is to skip all of the 'boring' bits of life. The scenes that used to happen in between major action clips in a film (or dramatic scenes if you are not a fan of action) are becoming as extinct as drive-in theaters. Take for example, Rocky 4. Have you ever seen Rocky 4? Okay, I know, it may have been a while, so here's a recap...

Rocky's mentor dies in the ring fighting a giant Russian boxer. And so Rocky, in spite of his over-the-hill-fighter condition, challenges him to a match. And just like in the other Rocky movies, what ensues is a fast forward of his many weeks of training. You see him go from pumping iron, to running through the streets. You see him swallowing raw egg yokes and wiping sweat off his brow. What you *don't* see are the moments in-between. When late at night laying in bed he was grieving his loss. When he was doubting his ability to do any of it. When he wanted to give up and go live in a shack on the beach for the rest of his life, or just end it all right now with a bullet.

Product designers and film makers have figured out that to keep you engaged they have to make things quicker, faster, greasier, and more exciting, and it has been a downward spiral for humanity ever since. Because in a regular paced life, the action, excitement, drama, and adrenaline rushes are few and far between. And in-between those peak moments is where life actually takes place. Where the day to day beauty happens. Beauty like sitting under a tree, just watching the traffic go by, or having a talk about 'nothing' with a friend.

If the culture has unconsciously programed you to want to skip those parts of life, you will never be able to build anything that lasts because these slow paced moments which make up ninety-nine percent of life are also where the immense amount of work you have to do to achieve something takes place. Attempting to skip from peak to peak in life makes you lose touch with many important parts of the process of achievement.

Because the film skipped it, you don't know that when Rocky was doubting himself, he chose to dig deeper and find connection to a source of love and nourishment within himself to give him the confidence to continue. You missed the moment when he was facing a challenge and he turned to his inner voice to receive inspiration. You missed his integration and grounding and how he fully processed his pain in order to clear his heart and mind and move forward.

The Rocky films show the first pillar of intuition - the pillar of vision and how Rocky takes action. But they (and other films, advertisers, news channels, and politicians), don't show you how the remaining pillars come into play. The pillars of connection, receptivity, and creativity. They don't show the *process* of creation and how to enjoy it.

The understanding that life and achievement is a process seems to be gone from Western culture. The idea of living moment to moment in simplicity and connection with nature (and at nature's pace) has become foreign. When you don't understand that life and creation are a process, not a series of peak action moments, it is easy to fall into a suicide Tuesday situation where you don't believe that what you want is achievable. Because you don't yet know how to cope with the detoxification of all the external stimulation and circling thoughts. By the end of this book, however, you will!

When life is not a series of adrenaline rush moments or peak experiences you might unconsciously think of yourself as a failure rather than an optimistic and inspired individual deeply engaged in the process of creating their vision. An individual that is doing the step by step work needed to attain something. So rather than really try and accomplish something, you may succumb to the temptation for escape yet again instead of facing that suicide Tuesday feeling and pushing past it.

There is a brilliant episode of The Simpsons where the electricity goes out and all the television sets stop working. Gradually, all the children start to trickle outdoors. At first they are blinded by the sunlight, and they walk around in a kind of oblivious zombie state. Then a ball goes bouncing past and the kids start to chase it. All of a sudden they remember how to play and how to imagine; how to laugh and get to know their own bodies and their friends. Then, of course, the electricity comes back on and they all go back inside to watch television again.

It is very difficult to escape the cycle of chasing peak experiences because the exposure to this kind of lifestyle probably started for you as a child. Like the rest of us, you were taught from very early on to expect life to be fast paced. Just think about Tom and Jerry chasing each other around. They might as well be Rocky and his Russian. Think about how the Roadrunner whips the Coyote's butt on those desert roads. They might as well be Anakin Skywalker and Darth Maul in the new Star Wars films. Real life isn't like that, and it creates immense amounts of suffering, unrealistic expectations, and a lack of motivation when you think it should be.

So be it movies, books, alcohol, drugs, sex, or other escapes, your imagination and ability to go from vision to creation and enjoy the process has been dulled. When your life doesn't flow like a stream of adrenaline rush moments, you may feel like something is wrong. But the reality is that that *wrongness* feeling is the wrongness of *expecting* your life to be like that. You need a complete shift in perspective. And yet, when you see it clearly, such an obvious one.

To achieve something real, you will have to walk up a mountain, step by dedicated step without the view changing dramatically. You will have to harvest the clay that builds the bricks. You will have to form the bricks and cook them. And then you will have to put them one on top of the other to build your house. Sometimes, you will even have to watch the rains come and wash it all away. You might have to start again from nothing and have to overcome the powerful temptation to hide behind the numb comfort of the familiar and not risk failure again. You will have to keep convincing yourself that walking your path of vision is better than hiding in the halls of numbness and fear, even when your drug of choice calls to you over and over again like a sick old ghost.

Journaling prompts:

1. What shows did you watch as a child? What do you like to watch (or read) now?

2. Looking at those shows or books, how have they unconsciously influenced how you think you should be living? How does that differ from how you are actually living?

3. How does the expectation or drive to live in that way prevent you from respecting your own desires, vision, and feelings? In other words, what kind of media-influenced negative self-talk do you have when you think about working towards your vision?

4. What are your 'vices?' What do you use to artificially create highs in your life? Here's a partial list of possibilities: the gym, gambling, Facebook, gaming, nicotine, coffee, narcotics, junk food, alcohol, picking fights with your family members, sex, drugs, etc. The idea isn't that anything is 'bad,' just that if it is being used as a way to escape yourself and avoid your fears, you might want to think about it.

5. How do you judge yourself, your life, and accomplishments when you compare them to that of the people you admire, be they real life heroes or fictional? What things do you tell yourself that you, 'should have accomplished by now,' or that you *'should* be like already?'

LONG-VIEW PERSPECTIVE

Below (in brief) is the cyclic, upward moving spiral, of building your pillars of intuition and becoming connected to your inner voice. It is offered to you here so you can better understand the process of creation. So that you can get comfortable and patiently sink into your process of transformation without expecting it to be a series of fireworks. You are in this process for the long haul. Stick with it, don't succumb to distractions, and your life will never be the same.

The upward spiral of the pillars of intuition:

1. **The Pillar of Vision:** Getting in touch with your pain, community, and inner warrior creates your passion and drive. You build a fire that urges you to push your boulder up that hill.

2. **The Pillar of Connection:** Your passion gives you the determination to overcome the oppressive voices of other people in your head. This creates a deeper sense of connection to a spiritual source and strengthens your relationships with others

in the physical world. This gives you the ability to overcome the suicide Tuesday effect.

3. **Pillar of Receptivity:** Your ability to be in positive relationships (both spiritually and physically) gives you the courage to receive new guidance. You can then let go of control and open yourself to support and direction from your inner voice. And to support from the people that show up to help you.

4. **Pillar of Creativity:** Building trust and an experience of co-creation (rather than control) allows you to be more vulnerable in your self-expression, allowing more and more authentic thoughts and ideas to flow through you from your inner voice. This self-expression allows you to employ ingenuity and act on your vision. It also allows you to achieve deeper levels of healing, insight and wisdom - by uncovering more and more of your old pain until you find the fertile silence in your heart.

5. **The Upward Spiral:** The pain and fertile silence that you uncover in yourself, once again, fuels your passion and builds your pillar of vision even higher and allows it to evolve in co-creation with your inner voice. And the spiral growth continues.

Understanding where you are ultimately headed will help motivate you to build your vision and strengthen your determination. In the chapter on connection you will learn more about coping with the suicide Tuesday effect and the feelings of meaninglessness and pointlessness that create it. In the chapter on receptivity you will learn to stabilize your connection to your inner voice for guidance and direction. And in the chapter on the pillar of creativity you will go much deeper into how detoxing your mind works and what you can do to ease the process.

For now, understand that having a vision and walking the path to attain that vision will not feel like a rush of adrenaline every moment of the day. It will ebb and flow just like everything else in this world, so make sure you remember that when your life doesn't feel like the movies, that it's okay - life *isn't meant to* feel like the movies!

You have put a vision into place, but it is easy to look at it and get depressed over not knowing how it is all going to come together. As you continue to progress through this book, the process of accomplishing your goals will become crystal clear. For now, simply keep in mind this upward spiral of building the four pillars of intuition, and then dig in and get ready to get your hands dirty doing some real work.

Take action:

Close your eyes and take a few deep breaths. Bring to mind the vision you have created for yourself. As you do that, become aware of the *feeling* of that vision in your body. Be aware of the positive emotions that are created in you as you think about it. Just be aware, having faith that as you connect to your inner voice, the way forward will become clear, even if right now you don't know how you are going to get from point A to point B. Journal about your experience.

DEPRESSION AND POINTLESSNESS

Expecting life to be a series of peak experiences or a constant state of emotional highs creates a gap in your mind between who you are and who you think you should be, and it is crucial to know that this gap is uncrossable. Because the images and desires you carry are not born from a connection to your inner voice. They are born of Hollywood, and by expectations placed upon you by your parents and other (often well-meaning) people, such as your teachers or clergy.

This gap is the result of thinking about who you think you *should* be, rather than who you *want* to be based on your own vision and your own experience in life. Who you *should* be is artificial and externally determined. Who you *want* to be has real emotional drive attached to it, not just guilt and shame over not being it. Who you *want* to be is aspirational. Who you *should* be is a source of great pressure and depression because you can never bridge the gap, and because you will never achieve *being* somebody else. You can be inspired by others, but you can never *be* anyone other than who you are.

The natural consequence of trying to bridge the *should* gap but never succeeding is a feeling of failure, often accompanied by a feeling of shame, hopelessness, and helplessness. And because hopelessness is such a terrible feeling, you look outside yourself to your drug of choice (be it food, television or an actual drug) for stimulation and comfort. But as already discussed, the high never lasts very long and next time you go looking for it, you need more of whatever it is to have the desired effect.

This is the cycle:

1. You fail to bridge the image of who you think you should be with who you are now.
2. This leads to hopelessness.
3. Hopelessness leads to seeking external stimulation from your drug of choice to distract you from that feeling.
4. This leads to the suicide Tuesday effect. Life starts to seem dim, creating feelings of depression and pointlessness, especially when thinking about following a vision for yourself.
5. These feelings start pulling you down, making you believe that whatever action you try to take will be meaningless.
6. This leads you to protecting yourself inside of a comfort zone cocoon.

The key to curing any dimness, meaninglessness, or lack of motivation you have is simple. You overcome the fear of failure. And there are two steps to that:

1. Recognize that when you are trying to live like other people tell you to live (be they your parents or Rocky), that you are doomed to failure. So you must change course to make *your own* vision of yourself your goal.

2. After that, you have to realize that creation is a process of learning and adapting. Even if you don't succeed at first, your inner voice will always guide you back on track based on what you learned from your experience.

You have to find the courage to live knowing that even if you fail and burn repeatedly that you can come back again and again until you succeed. You have to know that failure is inevitable as you walk the path to success. That there is no shame in failure but that there *is* shame in never really trying. In order to really get in front of this problem, you have to make your life your *own* adventure, knowing that most adventures are mostly about walking the trail of discovery, step by boring step, in order to build to peak moments of success at the end, if you are lucky.

There is not a single successful person out there who did not fail repeatedly before succeeding. And they still fail regularly, as they attempt new things. Simply put, successful people who find meaning in what they do are not afraid to make mistakes, learn from them, and keep going. They are not afraid of 'failure.' They see their attempts as science experiments. They use failed attempts to course correct and continue moving forward with curiosity and the rocket fuel of their own unique vision.

The fear of failure makes it incredibly hard to take sustained action without loosing momentum. To overcome this fear, you shift from pursuing who you think you *should* be (which is an impossible task), to pursing who you *want* to be (which is a completely achievable goal). You let go of trying to bridge the gap between who you are right now and who other people have taught you that you should be and instead, you learn to bridge the growing abyss between you and your inner voice, so that your vision can come from within. And by reading this book, you are doing it right now!

You are doing it even though sometimes the abyss between you and your inner voice seems more frightening than going around in circles, chasing pleasure and security in an ever changing world (aka living in your comfort zone). You are doing it even though it is easier to hide in the realm of the gods rather than rebuild your connection to your inner voice. You are doing it because you realize that your expectations of yourself are out of whack and that *not* achieving a life of peak moments should *not* be considered failure, and because now you better understand how following your vision is a process. And you understand that the work never ends - that after every peak you climb, there is another trail to walk, leading you up the next mountain.

Do you know what the reward is for a job well done? Another job. The work of life is never done. You never arrive at an unchanging and eternally blissful moment. So embrace failure! Embrace it as a sign that you have rejected numbness and are truly living your life. A sign that you are no longer living a comfort zone, realm of the gods kind of existence. A sign you should be proud of yourself.

Journaling prompts:

1. Ask yourself, 'Who do I think I *should* be right now that I'm not?' Your answer should be based on what other people's ingrained voices say. This can include comparisons that you make between yourself and other people. For example: when you say, 'I'm not as good as _____.'

2. Who do I *want* to be right now that I can choose to be or aspire to be instead of what I think I *should be?*

Example:

Who do I think I should be right now? Answer: Somebody who has published their books already (like the two other successful authors and teachers I'm friends with).

Who do I want to be right now? Answer: Somebody who persists against the challenges and works to see things through to the end no matter what delays I encounter along the way.

Take Action:

Set two reminders on your phone, one for midday and one in the evening saying: 'Who do I think I should be right now? Who do I want to be instead?' Any time you start to feel depressed, pointless or meaningless and your motivation tanks, ask yourself those two questions.

Journaling Prompt:

There is an ancient saying: When is the best time to plant a tree? The answer: 25 years ago. When is the second-best time? The answer is, *right now.* What tree are you going to plant right now, that you wish you had planted 25 years ago?

Take action:

Close your eyes and call the vision you created above into your mind. Now allow your fear of failure in. Allow the doubts and predictions of doom to roll in like a fog or a sand storm (or an army of zombies if you are feeling especially playful). How does it feel in your body to have your fear of failure roll over your vision in this way? What are the thoughts that go through your mind? What are the images of failure that you see in your imagination? Write them down.

Journaling prompt:

What do you currently consider yourself having failed at in your life? How can you start thinking about it as a part of a process? A scientific experiment from which you can learn, course correct, and try again?

BULLYING YOURSELF

Maybe you want to live your life free from the possibility of failing in your fight to accomplish your dreams and from the imagined devastation accompanying such failures. Maybe you prefer to succumb to all of your looping thoughts and helpless feelings and allow yourself to be bullied by them. Maybe you would feel better if you spent your life cowering to keep yourself safe and hidden.

Or… maybe you will realize that any imagined consequences you might suffer from sticking your neck out are going to be better than wasting away your life as somebody who never fulfilled their potential, or even tried. Even if you are afraid of all that effort being for nothing. Even if your inner demons are telling you that you can't do it - that you can't possibly achieve what you set out to achieve. That you will fail and be miserable and that you will be humiliated and made fun of. Even then… you *must* cultivate your vision and passion using your own pain to fuel your inspiration.

As somebody who may be living (or has had the experience of living) in the realm of the gods, choosing comfort over risk, you have the privilege of having a high perch from which to view the world. From that perch you are probably aware of the great injustices in the world in addition to the injustices you have suffered in your own life. You probably have the ability to see into people's hearts and empathize with their problems and their suffering. You might even be able to provide solutions for them, knowing instinctively what others can do to help themselves. Getting out there and helping those people is part of what building the pillar of vision is all about. It's about having the confidence to commit yourself to the process of trial and error as you make your way to the fulfillment of your vision, even if it is a slow step-by-fumbling-step kind of walk.

Building a powerful vision gives you the power of a storm. And you need to welcome that power even if you feel frightened that it will take over your mind and not the other way around. You need to stand on the edge of a cliff and shout out to the storm to come for you. Shout out to your inner demons to come and battle you. You need to slay them, burn with wrath from within and absorb their power knowing that no one can stop you.

To build your pillar of vision you need to get out from behind your daily tasks and position of comfort, stop thinking so much, and do what you know in your soul of souls to be beneficial for you and for others. Start a business, start a garden, start a blog or volunteer. It doesn't matter if you are not the next Deepak Chopra or Martin Luther King. There are millions of people taking action and offering their unique craft, love, and knowledge to anybody who will listen. Because they have a vision and a real desire to share the vision. Your voice and your power are needed among them!

If you have no idea where to start - start by doing something new, by removing distractions from your life, and owning your power. And to gather power for that journey, you need to realize that you are, when you are on your own, in fact, powerless.

Journaling prompt:

Write down 5 new things (things you have never done) that you could do that would move you towards accomplishing your vision.

Take action:
1. Stand up right now (even if you are in public), close your eyes and imagine yourself standing on a cliff overlooking the ocean. The ocean is raging with a storm. Call out to that storm to give you it's power. Imagine the full power of that storm entering your body and filling you up. Journal about your experience.
2. Choose at least 2 of the new things you can do from the list above and make a commitment to do them in the next 48 hours (or take a small step towards them). Circle the two you are going to act on.

COMMUNITY

Your power is not only needed among your community, your power is also generated by them. You are part of a collective. That collective is made up of a few famous people and hundreds of thousands of unknowns. People who, (like you if you are still building your pillar of vision), compare themselves to those at the very top and wonder if there is any point.

You may think you are less than these people, but what would *they* tell you you are? Would they say, 'Oh yes, you are certainly inferior to me!' with a haughty accent? Or perhaps they would they say, 'You know, I started out just like you, having no idea what I was getting myself into.'

Anybody can sit around grumbling about the 'edge' they don't think they have, or the privileges given to others. Few people have held the power of the storm and said, 'I am going to walk this path and no one is going to stop me!' What will *you* do?

Journaling prompts:
1. Who are/were the people at the top of your field (whatever it is) – activists, creators, artists, healers, writers, scientists you admire? Make a list of 5-10. If you don't have a specific field of interest, make this list a list of people you admire and want to emulate.

2. Do some research and find another 5-10 people who are doing similar work to that which you want to do who are *not* well known, but are doing the work nonetheless. These people are the real heroes.

Take action:

Put these names on a list and hang it on your wall. Print out images of their work and paste them up as well.

YOUR HEART PUMPS VIBRANTLY

One way to become energized again is to support all the other people in your community with *your* energy by inviting them into your heart and sending them power. When you make a conscious decision to offer your energy into this community of creators, you receive a burst of newfound energy and hope. When you know you have a community of people who are supportive and have the same intentions as you for the betterment of themselves and the world, your heart pumps more vibrantly and far further than you ever thought possible.

It's astounding and even counter-intuitive to think about, but when you start truly giving of yourself, the amount of energy you have increases exponentially. To become energized, you only need to close your eyes and connect – to feel yourself as part of this collective of inspiring souls, and send them your support. Doing this practice wholeheartedly, even without knowing the people you are supporting personally, or the entirety of the group you are a part of, makes you feel invincible. It gives you the understanding that you don't have to do it all. You only need do your (completely achievable) part. It's a relief.

And the best part - when you tune into that feeling of collective support and encouragement, you can also start asking for ideas and inspiration in return. You will receive the answers through your intuition and new opportunities will start coming to you. And when they do, you will take small, positive steps by saying yes to them.

You will start extending invitations and motivating people to work with you. You will take entrepreneurial risks. You will spread your ideas through a blog or a book, through research, artistic creation or through community activism (or anything else). You will work in your garden until your fingers ache in order to create something beautiful. You will not succumb to your fear of failure or any thoughts of meaninglessness and pointlessness.

Take action:

Close your eyes and tune into your artist's collective (whatever your art may be… painters, engineers, teachers, healers, gardeners… whichever it is for you *right now*). Feel in your body how the subtle energy of that collective exists. When you feel them, send nourishing energy and thoughts to the collective. Become aware how nourishing that collective, gives you energy in return. If it feels right to you, also ask the collective for inspiration, or an answer to a specific questions. Journal about your experience.

YOUR TOMBSTONE

When you can feel the support of a community, it is easier to reconnect with the pain you have within you and use it to dissolve the walls that have kept you out of your own castle. When your unconscious mind spits out how hopeless it all is and you get deflated yet again, just remember who you are emulating. Remember the community of heroes you are part of and are drawing inspiration from, and whether you are aware of it or not, also inspiring in return by offering them your support.

If they can do it, you can do it! There is nothing special about them. They simply decided that something in their life was greater than their own sense of security, convenience, safety, and comfort. That 'something greater,' is knowing there exists within them a higher purpose that needs to be expressed and shared with the world. Not knowing *how* they will achieve it, just knowing *what* it is and being willing to experiment and trust, and to let their vision evolve as *they* evolve.

The people who are your heroes are people of integrity who spoke the truth and had faith that they were doing the right thing. They made mistakes, they were scared, they were imperfect, but they spoke their truth and followed the path of their vision to innovate, create and inspire in their respective fields. Maybe they started an empire. Maybe they started a knitting circle. Whatever you desire, you can too! You must. Or when you die your tombstone will read: Here lies somebody who let the oppressive voices inside them keep them trapped – they could have been so much greater. Instead, if you take the actions you are scared of, it will say: Here lies a person who followed a calling. They fought in their own unique way to make the world a better place and left a legacy people are inspired to emulate.

If you are sitting around with no idea in which direction to go, look again. There is probably something you are saying, 'no' to. Some idea you are having about which you are saying to yourself, 'This idea can't be it.' Or you are saying, 'That won't work.' You may even be telling yourself, 'That's boring...' But it's not. It's actually the action you are supposed to be taking. It is the whisper of your inner voice that you are denying because it makes no sense or creates fear in your conscious mind.

However ridiculous your ideas might seem, take action in order to find out. Nothing will ever evolve without taking action on those ideas and exploring the unforeseen results of those actions. And if you are still having a hard time pinpointing an action to take, don't worry. We are going to cover overcoming all those negative voices in the next chapter and help you create clarity, so hang tight.

Journaling prompts:

1. What would you like your tombstone to say?

2. Do you have any ideas for acting on your vision which you are saying, 'no' to? About which you are telling yourself that they are not worth following? What are those ideas (write down at least 3)?

Take action:

Follow up on one of those ideas. Circle at least one you are going to follow up on. When are you going to do it?

THE WARRIOR ARCHETYPE

You can make your life as exciting an adventure as it feels like when you are watching your favorite show or reading the history (or mystery) books. The qualities of the warrior archetype (or Wisdom Warrior if you prefer) are readily accessible to you. When you embrace them, they make you uniquely qualified to act as a visionary and leader in your area of interest, whatever that may be.

You can take inspiration from the characters in your favorite books or television programs, turning that knowledge into a strength instead of an addiction and escape. You can move the world by calling on those character's strengths. Also, you can find real life heroes that you can draw inspiration from and learn their stories. People from the list you made earlier or other historical figures that acted from a clear place of vision - not just for themselves, but for the world at large.

As you look to stories for inspiration, ask yourself: Are the main characters in your stories saving the world? If so, get out there and save the world in *your own way*! Are they solving conflicts and bringing friends and neighbors back together? You too can make peace in your neighborhood. Are they people who solve mysteries? You can get a science degree. Are they explorers? What do *you* want to explore? Are they people who teach and inspire? Get out there and teach what you have knowledge of (even if you think you have nothing to offer). Out of 8 billion people, there are bound to be a few thousand who think what you have to say is worth listening to.

Journaling prompt:

By looking at the characters you are attracted to in fiction, you can learn about who you desire to be. So, who are the characters you like and identify with? How do they make decisions? What are the things they do? What kind of archetypes are they? Write down everything you know about them.

Take action:

Close your eyes and imagine you are one of your favorite characters. What are the emotions you feel when you are connected to them? Write them down.

IT DOESN'T MATTER

Creating a vision is not about taking a personality test to see what you are good at. It is about finding out what creates a feeling of aliveness in your body, even if that feeling is followed by a sinking feeling. That sinking feeling that is usually generated by thoughts such as, 'But I don't know how,' and, 'But I am not good enough.' The initial feeling is what matters and that is what you build your vision on.

It doesn't matter if you don't know how you are going to accomplish anything. It doesn't matter if you don't know how your vision is going to manifest. It's not about having clarity, it's about the power of *action* (however small, symbolic or confused) that no amount of inner knowing or thinking can create. So find one simple thing that you can do, and start there. Don't let any thoughts about how meaningless it is stop you, because you will never know the truth about anything unless you take action.

Some people think that because they can imagine what an experience is going to be like, that nothing can surprise them, or that the world has nothing new to offer them. It's nonsense! Just because you can imagine what it's like to go to India, or you have seen it on TV, it does not mean you have *any* idea what it's like. Or any idea what random experiences you will have happen to you if you go. A part of you may believe there is nothing new for you to experience in the world. But that's only because another part of you is keeping you 'safe' from the dangers of the unknown.

In order to feel that burning power and passion and in order to bring your gifts to the world, you have to bring yourself to do the things you may have become so good at avoiding. Let your pain fuel the passion that will help you overcome your doubts. And then take action after action after action in order to start bringing new experiences into your life. If you want internal change, you also have to make changes in your activities and your environment. You can't keep doing the same things and expect different results. You have to act differently to see and experience your life differently.

Journaling prompt:

Write down at least 5 things you could do to follow in the footsteps of your heroes (from the previous journaling prompt), no matter how small the steps seem. Keep this in mind for inspiration: "Do one thing every day that scares you!" ~ Eleanor Roosevelt

Take action:

Make a commitment to follow up on one of these steps in the next week. Which one is it going to be? Circle it above. If you choose, get somebody to hold you accountable to taking this step for yourself.

FUEL, EMBRACE, UNDERSTAND, REALIZE, BUILD

To summarize how you create your pillar of vision:

1. **Fuel** your fire with your pain and loss, using it to find what you are passionate about.

2. **Embrace** your inner hero based on the characters you admire and who you already know yourself to be.

3. **Understand** the power of action. Because no amount of knowing ever accomplished anything. Only action has.

4. **Realize** that you are part of a huge community of people that you can draw power from and that you can support in return - simply by closing your eyes and connecting.

5. **Build** your remaining pillars in order to establish a clear and ongoing partnership with your inner voice. Allowing your vision to evolve as you do.

Remember, building your pillar of vision isn't about knowing how you are going to accomplish anything. It is solely about knowing what it is you want to accomplish. Even if it takes you ten thousand years to do it. Even if you don't believe for a second that it is possible to accomplish. Even if it seems hopeless and you feel helpless to do anything about it.

LIGHTING YOUR INNER FIRE – SOME PRACTICAL SUGGESTIONS

The following is a list of actions you can take to help you build your vision and find out what you are motivated by:

1. **Create Conflict:** Find ways of getting that 'personal struggle' type of excitement into your life. Becoming an amateur martial artist or wrestler, for example. Joining any kind of competitive experience would be beneficial for you, though, from chess to tennis. Even if you lose terribly, you will see how not-horrible losing actually is and how much fun you can have along the way. Just be careful not to get addicted to winning.

2. **Micro-Steps:** Break up your long-term goals and dreams into manageable positive micro-commitments, and then act on them. Without pushing yourself to act on one of these daily micro-steps, you will never reach your destination. After all, the journey of a thousand miles starts by putting one foot in front of the other. Even if you only put 5 minutes a day towards your dream, that's good enough.

3. **Learn by Doing:** Take *action* regardless of your doubting self-talk. It's always better to create something imperfectly and continue working on it diligently, than

to continue hoping to create something in total perfection one day. You can only perfect your craft through dialogue and interaction with your audience and community. First, you must create something imperfect. Second, put it out in the world and invite feedback from other people. And third, you make improvements based on that feedback. And the cycle repeats.

4. **Experience, Don't Think:** When you think of an action step that you can take right away, don't let your doubting thoughts get in the way of simply taking it, even without having thought through all the possible consequences. No matter what assumptions you have about the results, until you take action, you don't really know how taking action is going to make you feel, what effect it will have on the world, or what doors will open up for you as a result.

5. **Text Message Check-Ins:** Have other people hold you accountable! Put together a group of people who want to better themselves and take determined steps forward. The need for external validation and accountability is one of the strongest motivators for taking action. Set regular weekly goals to connect with at least one person you trust who can act as your accountability angel. In person or phone is best, but even just a quick text check-in will do if you are super busy.

6. **Motivations:** Investigate and be clear about what you are motivated by and who you are doing your work for. Your motives don't have to be altruistic. You can do what you do to bring meaning, joy, financial wellbeing, and happiness to yourself and your family. Or you can take action, not for yourself, but for the sake of the world at large. Both are equally valid, so long as they come from a genuine place within you and you have a strong emotional connection to them.

7. **10,000 Year Goal:** Cultivate a wide-view awareness. Do you have a clear picture of your 10,000-year goal? What seed do you wish to plant with your actions that 10,000 years from now, will create the world (or galaxy for you sci-fi fans) of your dreams? If you are only thinking about your own lifetime, you are thinking too small!

8. **Who Do You Admire?:** Find a passionate leader that you admire (real or fictional). One that has warrior qualities to her/him. Tune in to this leader who persevered and rose up to the top in your field, and ask their spirit for inspiration and help. Literally – ask their spirit for guidance and receive your answers through your intuition (even if they are fictional). Study their life and find inspiration, motivation, and power. Build an altar or make a collage of their work that will inspire you daily.

9. **Contemplate This:** Our individual actions create ripples that affect billions of people beyond ourselves. Every person you touch, touches thousands, each of them touches thousands more and so forth… Until every person in the world is touched.

10. **Take Up The Torch:** When you don't challenge yourself, you don't get to have a clear connection to the insights that come from your inner voice and intuition. If you are not willing to take up the torch that your inner voice is charging you with, it's not going to waste it's energy trying to tell you how to move forward. Would *you* waste your time encouraging, inspiring and teaching somebody who never followed your direction? It's a two-way street. Make a pledge that you will follow your inner voice even if it makes you uncomfortable. That's when your inner voice will show back up in your life like a ton of bricks.

11. **Right Now:** Even if you have no idea how to attain your long-term vision, you will always know what to do right now. Ask yourself, 'What do I need to do right now, this second, in order to move myself towards my vision? Or towards *having* a vision.' The answer might be to get a cup of tea and relax. It might be to get your computer and learn to make a website. It could be anything. Trust it and follow it and you will learn to trust it in bigger and bigger ways.

Action Step:

Close your eyes and imagine: How will you touch people from now on, knowing that you are touching every person in the world each time you make a positive (or negative) impact on one individual life? Journal about it.

Journaling Prompt:

What do you want the world to look like in 10,000 years?

Take action:

Look back at your journaling notes and create **a brand new vision statement.** Write your vision statement on a large piece of paper or poster-board. Now add images to it - cutouts from magazines that you paste on the paper to make it more visual. Hang up your collage where you can see it every day.

Take action:

What do you need to do right now, this second, to move yourself towards your new vision? Whatever the answer is, get up and do it.

Are you still reading? Get up and do it!

FULL INTEGRITY

Look around you and you will see that life isn't about being comfortable. People are willing to endure all manner of difficulty to fulfill their calling. You can't avoid difficulty and attain a real connection to your inner voice. In fact, you will have to face major emotional and mental challenges to stay connected to it.

Just know that when you follow your chosen path with full integrity, whatever you accomplish is significant. It will give value to others and affect the world positively, even if you don't end up being well known for your craft outside of your community and clients. Ask yourself: Who would the great leaders be without all the people who built the steps they climbed to get there? The results you wish to see should be your motivation, not a desire for fame for fame's sake. And to be clear - there is nothing wrong with fame itself when that fame supports your visions and goals.

Along the way you will be supported by innumerable souls and you will, in turn, support others. It is only together that we will ultimately accomplish anything. Not by seeking the recognition for it. It is only by allowing your community to help you course-correct and improve that you will eventually arrive at your chosen destination. The people along the way will be your mirrors. They will be your productive critics. They will be your cheerleaders. They will be your inspiration. And their wellbeing will be your motivation. It is only through relationship that you can grow as the world around you challenges and inspires you in new and unexpected ways.

You barely have a fraction of the information about what you are doing, or where you might fit in the bigger cosmic picture. You have to follow the breadcrumbs by seeing where your actions and inner voice lead you. If you never take action, you will never make a difference; not in your own life, and not in the lives of others. So whenever you encounter the wall of doubt, helplessness or despair, thinking you won't really be able to change anything, remember:

1. Ask yourself what you think you *should* be right now? And then shift your aspiration to be what you *want* to be instead.

2. Be honest with yourself about what you want to be. Be aware of any self-censorship of the answer in the moment you ask the question. You will be the happiest and most authentic version of yourself that way (and happy people make the world a better place to live).

3. Remember that who you want to be in any given moment can be different. It could be related to the specific situation you are in, and not necessarily your long-term goals. The answer that comes to you might be that you want to be somebody who takes a break when they need it. It might be, 'I want to be somebody who takes five deep breaths instead of eating the extra French fries on my plate.'

4. Ask yourself, 'What can I do right now, this second, to take a step towards my goal of who I want to be?'

5. When you get your answer, take action no matter what. Trust it and follow it without looking back.

Journaling Prompt:

What is the primary discomfort you will have to face to follow your vision? How will you motivate yourself to face that discomfort?

STICKING YOUR NECK OUT

If you are still building the pillar of vision, you might find yourself sitting at home and ignoring your inner voice. And if you are, you are robbing yourself of a life of true adventure and true purpose. Deep down you are desperate to express that call. And now you can. You have created a vision and you have found motivation in the pain you have suffered in life. You have learned:

1. Taking action regardless of your greatest fears is the most crucial key to success.
2. There is no growth without challenging yourself and leaving your places and habits of comfort behind.
3. Your initial vision for yourself is exactly that - an initial vision.
4. Your vision will change, grow, and evolve as *you* do, and as your community challenges you to. Your role is to allow this process to unfold.
5. To treat failure as inevitable and as an adventure rather than a devastating event.

To build your pillar of vision, let the barriers of numbness and sorrow break down and allow any pain and rage within you to unfold like a thousand stories. They will fuel your warrior nature into action. When you connect deeply to your own pain it helps you connect to the great and overwhelming compassion and love that lives in the very fabric of your being.

Can you bring that power forward? Can you surrender your life in service and embrace the discomfort that this will inevitably generate? Can you do it even though you could choose to live your whole life in relative comfort, without ever having to stick your neck out? Can you do it because even if through your actions you bring happiness to only one soul, it will have been worth it? As through that single soul you will have touched the whole world, even if you don't realize it?

Working on your vision is a privilege. It means you have choice in life. What are you going to do with your ability to choose? What micro-action steps are you going to take today? Follow the first thing that comes to mind and don't look back when the voices of doubt and helplessness start hounding you. As encouragement, try out this timeless childhood rhyme: Sticks and stones can break my bones, but names (and mental doubts) can never hurt me (unless I listen to them).

And when you find yourself overcome with those mental doubts, as you invariably will at times, focus on building your pillar of connection, where you learn how to connect to a source of love and nourishment within, and learn to overcome the fear of isolation.

Journaling Prompt:

Who are the people you know or have met that you believe have a strong pillar of vision. What can you learn from them?

Take action:

Ask the people you know who have a strong pillar of vision for advice on building yours. Reach out to at least one person right now. Journal about the advice they give.

BUILDING THE PILLAR OF CONNECTION

THE PILLAR

The gift of the pillar of connection is in building a direct channel to a source of spiritual nourishment deep within you. A source of nourishment that won't let you down or judge you. A source that is full, abundant, and overflowing with faith in your ability to accomplish your work in the world. A source of true love and worthiness.

Building the pillar of connection helps you find your inner voice because without a connection to this spiritual source of nourishment, other people's voices will drown out your own. You will give up your own truth and your own *rare intelligence* to receive affection and 'love' from somebody outside yourself. You will be afraid of conflict and rejection, and you will shut out your inner voice when it is trying to guide you to express your authentic self.

Building a connection to a spiritual source of nourishment and love also allows you to build positive relationships founded on honesty, compassion, and empathy. This is what is meant by having rare intelligence - the ability to create heart-lifting connections while being aware of the same deep longing for love in every soul around you. It means that you will always have words of wisdom, an empathic touch, and heart-felt tenderness to offer people you meet on your path, balanced with a sense of individuated self.

People who exemplify this rare intelligence are like Mother Theresa and the Dalai Lama. So deeply connected to love and wisdom in their own being, they know each and every one of us emanate from the same source, but they are still strong enough to say 'no' to oppression. Not all people who have developed this pillar are leaders of that magnitude, however. They are also the people around you every day; the people who organize your neighborhood block parties, your friends who are learning how to use Non-Violent Communication in their relationships, and the local small business owner who is adopting a collectivist approach to management.

Being in connection to the love-source within you means that all you create in the world is based on love and collaboration. It means you embody love wherever you go, instead of seeking it wherever you go. It allows you to express yourself honestly and yet compassionately, creating community and harmony rather than conflict. The power of connection is the power of loving presence balanced by strength and integrity, where your words, deeds and wisdom flow directly from your inner voice into the world.

Take action:
Close your eyes and take a few deep breaths. Imagine being connected to an unlimited source of nourishment and love within you. What does that feel like in your body? Describe the feeling in your journal.

Journaling prompt:
In what life situations do you tend to look for external validation before acting?

THE CHALLENGE: WHEN IT FEELS SAFE

When your pillar of connection is still being built, you may find that you know what your inner voice says, but that there are too many doubts and contradicting voices in your mind. When this happens, you may choose not to speak or follow you inner wisdom, but instead stay silent and go with the flow.

The modern-day culture of speed and competition doesn't offer space to create genuine, authentic and loving conversations. And yet the thing that most people crave is for the people around them to slow down and show up as open, safe, respectful and supportive beings, which provides an atmosphere conducive to self-expression. When you feel safe and connected, your brilliance can shine through. When you feel afraid, you hide that brilliance and try desperately to fit in.

If you are still building your pillar of connection, you probably avoid situations where you may have to defend yourself or your position. This could include speaking up when you might contradict the status quo, question authority, risk hurting someone's feelings or create a confrontation, because the result can be conflict. And when in conflict, many people resort to some form of violence (whether they realize it or not) in order to defend their position – verbally, mentally, or even physically.

When you speak your truth in these situations, but lack a pillar of connection, you risk the pain of isolation and separation, and it is this fear of isolation and separation resulting from conflict that controls you. It is not the fear of conflict in itself that is the problem, but rather it is the potential consequence of *feeling isolated* as a result that you fear. To counter this fear of isolation and find your inner voice again, you must build a connection to an internal source of nourishment and love.

As you undertake this journey to authentic connection, you will start to naturally respect yourself as a person with your own strong voice and perspective. You will also be able to respect and honor other people's differences and processes. The kind of honoring of others that can only come from an internal honoring of yourself first. An honoring that is sourced in your own conviction, curiosity and willingness to learn, grow and serve. The kind of honoring, you probably never received as a child.

Journaling prompts:
1. What situations do you avoid for fear of feeling isolated?
2. What situations in your past can you identify that caused you to feel isolated?

Take action:

Do this in your journal or get a separate piece of paper or poster board. Title it: I Honor Myself For... After that, make a collage or make a list of at least 10 things that you honor yourself for (making a collage is the more powerful approach).

RECIPROCATION

When building your pillar of connection, what you need most is a safe environment where everybody respects each other's thoughts and ideas in a collaborative way. An environment where no one is threatened by other people's genius and everybody can thrive. You may crave this kind of environment so much that you try to create it artificially by avoiding confrontation – even if the people around you don't reciprocate.

But if people in your environment don't reciprocate, you may find yourself falling deeper and deeper into a hole where people expect you to be a certain way. A way that is likely contrary to who you really are and what you believe in. You are then more likely to shut down your own inner wisdom and need for self-care. As these kinds of social agreements solidify, you find yourself more obligated to be that person. The more that time passes, the more these agreements get set in stone, and the more stuck you become.

In these situations where you may feel unsafe, you adopt the thoughts and judgments of other people over your own because you are trying to create the respectful, peaceful, and connected environment that you so crave. It is very ironic: in order to avoid isolation and separation you might create an artificial persona that makes other people feel comfortable and takes care of their egos. The result, though imperfect and ultimately false, gives you a sense of temporary safety. Ultimately, however, a sense of separation and isolation solidifies anyway, because you can't bring your authentic self into full expression in this kind of environment.

Journaling prompt:

In your life, who are you afraid of getting into confrontations with and why?

THE ROAD TO OPPRESSION

Tracing your steps back to your authentic inner voice can seem difficult, if not impossible, when you don't feel safe and in connection, but rest assured that it is possible. One of the roadblocks you will face is that when you start to live from an internal source of nourishment and love, it could mean having to renegotiate your relationships; perhaps even key elements of your life, like your marriage or career. It is possible that you are so deeply committed to a false version of yourself that your entire life could fall apart when you start expressing your authentic inner voice or even just the true questions and curiosities that live within you. Hopefully, your case is not so extreme, but for some people, it is.

When you don't have a strong pillar of connection, one of the reasons might be that you don't have a *balanced* empathic ability. Everybody is born with empathic ability and in remembrance of oneness - to an infant, everything is interconnected. The natural path of a child's growth is to maintain that awareness while balancing it with a healthy dose of individuation and spiritual identity. Which is to say - the identity that you organically develop when you are connected to your inner voice and surrounded by unconditional love. An awareness of being both the part *and* the whole (or the finger *and* the brain as described in the second chapter, The Path of Mastery).

Most children don't get the support they need to grow up in this balanced way. Instead, they are forced to wear an identity created for them by their environment. The majority of children succumb to that oppression and live their lives in struggle and pain, and not even aware they are in struggle. There are some children, however, who rebel and don't succumb to this conditioning; children who try and hold on to their true selves at all costs. This rebellion against the standard mold and the rejection of authenticity by their environment may often times, however, lead to an imbalance.

If you were one of these children who refused to accept oppression, the path of rebellion may have taken you to an extreme. You became either empathic without full awareness of your individuated self or narcissistic without awareness of others. If you are reading this book, it is most likely the former. The child who chooses to maintain their awareness of unity consciousness and reject the awareness of their own body and emotions does so because they see the harm that separation consciousness does and they don't have the tools to cope with the pain of rejection and their fear-based environment. To cope with the pain caused by an un-aware environment, the child takes shelter in the spirit world and becomes more aware of energy outside themselves than they are of the energy within themselves.

The child who chooses separation consciousness (the narcissist) and rejects any awareness of the other also does so because they wish to disconnect from the source of their pain, but contrary to the empath, they hide inside their own head in a kind of emotionally catatonic state. The unbalanced empath hides from their pain outside themselves, the narcissist hides inside themselves. Both are disconnected from their own wholeness and from a true source of nourishment. Ultimately, for both of these children, the result can be numbness and an inability to find fulfillment, balance, self-expression and true connection.

It is interesting to note that there is a good reason unbalanced empaths and narcissist often choose to have each other as partners. It is because they are opposites on a spectrum and are both trying to get back to center, however unconscious that desire might be. The empath must learn that having an identity, enjoying one's body, having positive, 'selfish,' emotions, and pleasurable experiences are all part of a balanced and healthy living experience. The narcissist must reclaim their awareness of the interconnected web of life.

When you build your pillar of connection, you start to feel safe again in your own body. You start to embrace the pleasure of being you, knowing that there is an unconditional source of love and that you were born to be your authentic, supported and joyful self. When you find your balance - aware of the whole and also a *self* within the whole, that is the beginning of becoming a true mystic.

Being able to intuit what other people are experiencing and feeling can be both a strength and a liability. Being an empath can make you insightful, wise, loving, and caring when balanced with the ability to take good care of yourself and boldly follow your intuition. It also has the potential to take you down the road of oppression because it allows you to avoid confrontation by prioritizing and accommodating the people around you over honoring your own needs, emotions, and ideas. When empathic ability is used in this fear-based way, however, it only serves to perpetuate feelings of isolation on both sides of the equation. It also stunts growth.

In the chapter on the pillar of creativity we will further discuss why childhood conditioning and trauma creates an imbalanced empathic ability. We will also discuss how, to some degree, maintaining your empathic ability despite the difficulty it can bring may have been a way of protecting yourself. And we will discuss how unbalanced empathic ability creates unwanted head chatter and discover ways of coping and clearing that chatter.

There is a true gift in being a balanced empath with both an awareness of your own body and emotions and a compassionate outlook on the emotions and circumstances of others. This awareness can take you down the road of true leadership when it is used to bring people together and share your wisdom. When you reconnect with your own true spiritually sourced identity, you naturally step into a leadership role. You are moved by a desire to bring people together; encouraging authentic self-expression instead of competing with or belittling others. You create connection and community in service to something greater. This can only be done, however, when you are connected to that deeper source of nourishment and love within, when you are willing to confront any feelings of isolation inside of you, and when you are willing to face that being your true self may bring change to your existing relationships.

Journaling prompt:

If you were to *be* the person underneath your persona (be your spiritually sourced identity), without a fear of isolation and separation generated by conflict, which relationships and what situations in your life might have to change and how?

Take action:

List at least 5 things you can do to honor the person who you are underneath your persona. These could be places to go, things to do or changes to make. When you are done, circle at least one of these actions and commit to making it a reality in the next 48 hours.

BRINGING PEOPLE TOGETHER

The problem you may be facing if you don't have a sturdy pillar of connection isn't that you have a need to avoid conflict, but rather the avoidance of conflict is a *symptom* of the feelings of isolation buried within you that conflict could stir up. Essentially, you might avoid confrontation and self-expression because you assume somebody will get hurt and respond by pushing you away (or threatening to). Thus creating the experience of isolation.

The reason you know to avoid these situations is because of past experiences of being pushed away or punished for simply being who you are (or not being the way others wanted you to be). And because, chances are, your authentic gifts were not recognized, nourished and welcomed as they should have been when you were a child, creating the experience of malnourishment, disconnection and isolation.

When you develop a strong pillar of connection it will allow you to bring your full self-expression to the community. You will be able to express yourself with the intention of bringing people together in the interest of mutual benefit and sharing instead of competition. You will be able to hold that energy throughout a conversation regardless of opposing views or even abusive behavior on the other side.

Having a strong pillar of connection allows you to have *rare intelligence:* Deep connection and harmony inside yourself that you are able to bring forward and share as a gift with other people. To anchor this rare intelligence, you need to solidify the understanding that your strength is in creating connection and community, not in learning how to blend in or 'win the fight'.

Journaling prompt:

What does rare intelligence mean to you? How could it be expressed in the context of your own life?

AN EPIDEMIC

Many of us were taught from an early age that to get ahead and feel powerful we must instill fear in others to control them. That we need to be something other than our authentic selves to be worthy of the love and respect of friends and family. This mostly stems from the use of violence, shaming, and punishment to instill discipline, and from playground bullying and hazing. It can also be caused by 'innocent' teasing and body shaming, or a competitive atmosphere in school and in sports. It is no wonder the feeling of isolation is practically an epidemic in today's society.

Yet another irony in this situation is that so many people feel this isolation and separation and yet most people are not comfortable discussing it. Rarely does anybody give themselves or the people around them permission to acknowledge it and to just be who they are. We need people with strong pillars of connection to help heal this horrible imbalance in our culture. People who are willing to build their pillar and become natural empathic bridges. People who have the strength of an internal connection to call on when they need to say 'no' to properly honor themselves.

It's complicated, to be sure, as 'just be who you are' is often touted as a cure-all. The truth is that there are many voices in the mind and not all of them are voices with good intentions. Figuring out who you are amidst the chaos and being an authentically good person takes time and effort. It takes developing a razor-like awareness to separate the experience of your authentic self from the thoughts in your mind. It takes an understanding that any ill-intentioned mental voices are merely the result of years of repression of the innate good within you. It takes trial and error and often times, a dark night of the soul. Where you dive into that internalized feeling of isolation and come out the other side as bonded to your inner voice.

Rising up as a leader of rare intelligence takes daily, moment to moment, practice to continuously re-focus your attention on all that is good and right about you. Underneath it all, everybody moves to the same tune – the tune of love and nourishment. It is possible for everybody to live there. It is possible for you to help create that world through your natural empathic ability and an internalized sense of connection to an infinite source of nourishment and love within you.

Journaling Prompts:
1. Who do you personally know that you feel is especially affected by the culture of isolation and separation?
2. What entities (work environments, schools, and other organizations) do you know that are also affected by this epidemic?

Take action:

Reach out to a person that you know who is deeply affected by the culture of isolation or is a part of one of those environments. Ask them about what it's like for them. Tell them you were thinking about them and just wanted to express your love. Example: 'Hi, I was thinking about you and the company you work for today. It seems like it's a difficult place to really be yourself in, is that correct? How does that affect you?'

Who are you going to call? When are you going to call? What are you going to say? Make a plan.

A WILLINGNESS TO ENDURE

Life isn't about making other people feel good! If all you do is try and make people feel 'good,' then you become a drug, and they become addicted to you providing them with validation. They become dependent on you to feel comfortable and you don't really change anything, you just avoid truths that would help both of you grow. Wanting to communicate without causing any pain or discomfort causes a kind of paralysis. You have to be willing to trust your underlying good intentions and sense of connection, regardless of how other people react to you. You have to learn how to communicate from a place of connection to your own source of nourishment and love.

If you reflect for a while on humanity, you will quickly see that people are willing to endure all sorts of hardships in order to feel proud, accomplished and powerful. They endure no matter how uncomfortable they must be in order to get there. You too must be willing to face discomfort if you are to evolve, grow and manifest your dual goal of living from your truth whilst living in peace and harmony with other people, and you have to be willing to face conflict on your way there. The solution is in focusing on loving people, not on preventing them (or yourself) from experiencing any negative emotions, which is impossible. You can't keep the peace and create a better world when you lie, regardless of how people's egos take it. You just need to find the most loving and compassionate way to tell the truth, and this is a skill that can be learned.

Sometimes that truth will lead to situations where you will have to call on your internal pillar of connection to support you. Situations where no matter how much the other person may try and bully you, you must hold steadfast against the fear of isolation. You will have to remember that no matter how isolated they are trying to make you feel, that you have a source of unlimited love and connection within you that fills you up. It's uncomfortable, but a necessary step in your evolution. How to do this will be covered below.

One problem you may face is that your life circumstances might be such that you are dependent on certain people to take care of you (a partner/provider or an employer). It might be that as you start coming out of your shell, they will try and hold power over you and you will have a real crisis of survival on your hands. In that case, while building a sense of connection within and learning how to speak your truth from a place of power and interconnection, you will also need to build a physical safety net: a place to live and somebody who can help feed you (or you and your children if need be) in case of emergency.

For some people, there is a real danger that being themselves will turn their world upside down. The danger being that the people who are accustomed to being taken care of by them choose to reject rather than respect them. The fear for most people who are at the beginning stages of building their pillar of connection is, naturally, that they live in this kind of dire situation and that they will be rejected and punished for being themselves. The truth is, you will never know if that's true until you try. Either way, if you have this fear, creating a safety net of some kind should allow you to take some steps forward and make you feel more empowered as you start to actively construct a new, more authentic life for yourself.

For now, let's assume your situation is not this dire and let's talk about the best ways to begin having empowered conversations.

Journaling prompt:

How are you like a drug to somebody in your life (more concerned with making them feel good than with the truth)? What is one small step you can take to reclaim truth in that situation?

Take action:

Do you have a need to create a safety net in your life (the safety net could be emotional as well as physical)? Make a list of steps you can take to create it. And then take one of those actions when you feel ready.

HEALTHY CONVERSATIONS

An internal feeling of connection allows you to offer your perspectives while recognizing that your perspectives are just as flawed and imperfect as other people's perspectives and to have conversations where the intention is for both of you to feel better in the end. Meaning, you are not shaming them or blaming them with your truth. Rather, you are having a conversation where you strive for mutual betterment.

Healthy conversations shouldn't have winners and losers. They should only have engagement, respect, and at the end, mutual understanding. Approach these conversations with a point of view that sees (if not the positive aspects of the truth itself) the positive outcomes that could come from the potential collaboration. Seeing yourself as part of the conversation whether you are right or wrong is the key. Regardless of how disappointed or challenged somebody might be.

In an ideal world, everybody would want healthy conversations. They would pause, look at you, and give you time to breathe, collect your thoughts, and make your remarks. We do not live in an ideal world yet. And the people around you may have become accustomed to you not sharing your wisdom, so they ignore you and don't seek it. If there is a competition for power (be it your marriage or your work), people may get very passionate, speak fast, and try to be the only ones that get heard.

The only way for you to really affect change if these situations are out of balance for you is to bring a seed of collaboration and respect to your relationships and *stick with it*. Through determination, and courageously cultivating an internal sense of connection and love. It's not about developing confidence – it's about feeling connected. It's not about insecurity or somehow feeling stronger and being able to be confrontational, it's about building a community of equals to better serve ourselves and others.

People get scared and defensive when living in a competitive environment. The only sustainable answer to this problem is to radiate a feeling of care and community. This is not done by covering up hard truths. Quite the opposite, it's done by handling difficult conversations and conflict while at the same time knowing that the community will never abandon any one of its members even though conflict and difficulty exist.

The key is to be open to a process rather than stay entrenched in your hurt, opinions and perspectives. It is only in engaging in true, community-oriented dialogue that wholeness and genius can be found. If you trust in your inner knowing and in the collaborative process, you can bring yourself back from out of the shadows and be a true connector, speaking the words of wisdom you have with a powerful, authentic voice.

You can help create this kind of world by first building the pillar of connection within yourself. By doing the Being in Connection practice (you will learn it further on) and building an internal community of spiritual caretakers and supporters to turn to when you are feeling isolated and scared and when you don't know how you are going to get from point A to point B. It is when you build the pillar of connection within, that you can start building relationships based on respectful connection outside yourself as well.

Take action: Peace for Everyone Meditation

What if there was no danger of you ever being abandoned? Close your eyes and imagine that the world is at peace. That there are plenty of resources to go around and people were respected for exactly who they are no matter what. Imagine that you were always taken care of by your community with love and nourishment. What does that feel like in your body? Describe your experience in your journal.

Journaling prompt:

How can you help create this kind of world?

CULTIVATE AN INNER FEELING OF CONNECTION AND COMMUNITY

Cultivating curiosity:

Curiosity is a key ingredient in having healthy conversations. Curiosity and a genuine desire to learn and grow. When you can enter a conversation with curiosity instead of fear, you will find your voice. When you can see that the conversation isn't about right or wrong but about exploration, you allow the spirit of collaboration and mutual benefit to thrive. When you embrace curiosity as a motivator, you will learn that other people's voices are no less and no more accurate than yours; that no one has the whole truth, and every question asked, and every perspective offered, is valuable. If you bring this attitude to your conversations, it will rub off on those around you (even if it takes a while).

Journaling prompts:

1. What am I curious about in the present moment?
2. What was I curious about 10 years ago?
3. What was I curious about as a child?

Cultivating a feeling of inner connection:

When you are cultivating a feeling, it takes more self-awareness and practice than simply thinking about something. As you have probably already experienced in your life, positive thinking can only get you so far. You must make deeper changes on the non-verbal levels of your consciousness in order to become the authentic you.

Outlined here is a practice called Being in Connection. You can do it whenever you feel the need for support and grounding, or to re-establish your connection to yourself. You can do this practice anywhere and with anybody around you (without them ever knowing what you are up to) as once you are familiar with it, it only takes a few minutes to do.

1. Close your eyes (if you are alone) and focus on your navel as a primal symbol of connection, while taking a few deep breaths.
2. Imagine that your navel is connected to a golden umbilical cord, but don't look to see what it connects to yet on the other end.
3. Receive all the nourishment and love you need from this cord – physically, emotionally, mentally, and spiritually. Notice how your body and mind change (even in the smallest of ways) as you do this.
4. After a few minutes of receiving, in your imagination, follow the umbilical cord to see who or what it is attached to on the other end and find out where your source of nourishment is (recognizing that it might be different each time you do this practice). Feel and honor this connection for as long as you can.

5. If you have any specific questions or requests, ask them of whoever, or whatever, is on the other side of the cord.

6. Take that feeling of connection with you as you go about your day. Whenever you are feeling depleted, remember it.

You can do this practice any time you feel isolated or lack the energy to speak up. While simple and short, it is quite profound and will give you a much-needed connection to a community of higher consciousness beings that you will find on the other side of the umbilical cord. By doing this practice again and again, you will build a network of spiritual nourishers and caretakers to turn to when you need a feeling of connection.

Take action:

Close your eyes, take a few deep breaths, and do the Being in Connection practice now. You can also download the audio from the website and use it to practice. Journal about your experience.

SAMPLE CONVERSATIONS

Below are a few practical suggestions and examples of scenarios where you might start to change the way you interact. The examples are slightly humorous on purpose. The idea is to empower you with a direction to go in as you replace the examples with your own words and style.

1. **Create comfortable environments that give you the space you need to fully express yourself:**
   A. Seek out one-on-one conversations instead of trying to make yourself heard in large group settings. Trying to draw attention to yourself in large groups can be stressful at first, especially when other people might jump in over you.
   B. If you are ready for the large group self-expression challenge, then you can express to your counterparts exactly what kind of environment you thrive in, and what you need from them.

Example: Hi everybody, I want to let you all know that it makes a huge difference to me when you give me a little extra space to express my thoughts. I'm not like most of you extroverts, and I don't think and speak at the same time. Usually, I need to think before I speak, so having the time to slow down means a lot to me. It would even be helpful if you took the time to ask me directly what I'm thinking or invite me to speak at a specific time rather than expecting me to just jump into the conversation spontaneously.

2. **In order to help other people feel safe and bring out the communitarian within them you can:**
   A. Figure out what their biggest fear is and let them know that you are not going to make it a reality.

Example: Hey co-worker, I have some ideas about that project we're working on that I'd like to share. I want you to know that while they are different than some of your ideas, my true intention is to find a way that we can collaborate to make the project even better. Are you willing to think outside the box with me and be open minded about it? Oh, and in case you're wondering, I'm way too busy at home to want that promotion that I know you're after, so no need to worry about having to compete with me.

B.   Lead with your vulnerability.

Example: Hello my good friend, it's been a long time since we talked. I know it has a lot to do with the fight we had. I want you to know that I sincerely regret it and feel extremely sad that we couldn't work it out in a compassionate way. If you're still angry with me, I understand, but I want you to know that I have every intention of being humble in this interaction and doing whatever it takes to restore our friendship. I don't know how to do it but I'm willing to show up and listen if you're interested. I'm feeling really vulnerable telling you all this, but keeping it inside and having to avoid each other like we do, is even more painful.

C.   Authenticity Heals.

Example: Hey sweet husband, so I've been thinking about a lot of things lately and I really want to share them with you. Can we make some very specific time for me to tell you about them? I want to take turns talking when we do it. I don't want you to interrupt until I'm done. And when I'm done, I want you to tell me how awesome my ideas are before you share yours.

When you lack confidence, you can ask a trusted ally to act as a witness. Somebody you can rehearse with or who can help mediate a conversation.

Journaling prompt:

Pick the types of conversations from the above list that are most relevant to you. Who will you have those conversations with? What will you say?

Take action:

Give yourself a time frame for when you are going to have one of those conversations. List 3-5 actions you need to take in order to make that conversation happen.

THE PEOPLE WHO HURT YOU

We all want love and we all look for it in the ways we've been taught how. You, your parents, the bullies at school, the abusive people at university or in your work environment; even the drug lords and the Nazis. Everybody wants safety, acceptance, love, self-expression, peace, freedom, and connection. We come into this world with an innate comprehension that these things are our nature. But due to our helpless nature as infants, we get conditioned to look for these emotions outside ourselves. And that is a very disappointing journey. One where we often lose our internal sense of connection to love and nourishment.

There is absolutely no way that anybody outside of you can provide you with the pure calm that your own innate connection to your true nature can provide. And yet you still have an unconscious place where you are looking for it. You may project it onto your spouse. You may still be trying to get it from a parent, even if they are deceased.

Building the pillar of connection begins with letting go of the expectation of getting unconditional love from outside yourself. By opening your eyes to see the flawed, blind search for love that is in every person. Especially the people who hurt you. Especially the people who you wanted pure love and safety from but who hurt you. Especially the ones who thought they *had to* hurt you to educate and discipline you. Which was never true, they just didn't know any better.

Like most of us, you probably grew up in a culture of punishment and reward. A culture where whoever gets to inflict the most pain on the other gets to control the other's behavior. When you punish a child, you inflict physical or emotional pain on them with the hope that they will behave in the way you want. When you inflict emotional distance on your lover you do so to make them 'give you the love you want'.

When a person steals, robs or murders they do so because they were afraid for their own life in some way. Inflicting more pain on them simply perpetuates the cycle of violence. People (whether children or adults) don't need to be violently subdued. They need to be lovingly and patiently fed. And they need to always know that there is a place of safety and loving nourishment for them in the world. Holding that intention is the only way you will ever help create a world of harmony where we don't have to be afraid of each other.

It's difficult to start letting the people you resent for having caused disconnection and an internalized experience of isolation off the hook. But wouldn't you want to be let off the hook? After all, you too have hurt and manipulated people. All because of your search for love and safety, and because you didn't know any better. By each of us building our own pillars of connection, we can together stop the cycle and build a world of connection instead.

Take Action:

Do the Forgiveness Ritual in the appendix of this book.

Journaling prompts:

1. Try and remember a time when you were at your lowest point in terms of your pillar of connection. A time when you were mostly looking for love, nourishment and validation outside yourself. Describe that time.

2. Did anybody in your childhood think they had to hurt you, shame you or otherwise isolate you in order to teach you or discipline you? Write about those

people and how they made you feel.

3. What are some of the things you have been made to believe that you should be punished for?

4. How can you help stop the cycle of violence and isolation in your own surroundings?

THE DARK NIGHT OF THE SOUL

When you finally reach the understanding that everybody is blindly fumbling around this world looking for love, a very important thing happens. The dark night of the soul begins. The dark night is a grief process where you let go of those external things that you thought would bring you love, nourishment and connection in the outside world. You let go of what you were taught and find yourself surrounded by darkness - by a feeling of not knowing who you are anymore. But the secret blessing of that darkness is that the darkness is actually fertile soil.

To build the pillar of connection you need to let go of your hope of getting nourishment and love from anybody in the external world without first finding it within yourself. When you let go of finding love outside yourself, you will find that you have become a seed again. A seed planted in lush, moist and nutrition-rich soil. That's when the magic really begins, because you start to sprout the roots of the real, authentic you, especially when you learn to properly *receive* the nutrients you need from that soil. Once you find that source within you, you can *share* love with others instead of *getting* it from them.

And then something even greater happens! You grow the roots and shoots of your authentic self and you start to see the world as a place *full* of love instead of the chaotic and difficult-to-attain-love place that it once seemed to be. You become a beacon of love and, as a result, the people around you start to reflect that back to you. You begin to see the world as a place where you can dabble in love and self-expression to your heart's content and not have to worry about feelings of isolation. Not worry about how people might hurt you and reject you for being your authentic self and speaking your truth. Not because those people don't exist, but because you are not looking for validation from them anymore. You can see that they do what they do only because of their own desperate and miserable search for safety, love and self-expression, disconnected from their own pillar of connection to nourishment and love.

Journaling prompt:

What does it feel like to let go of your external sources of love, nourishment and validation?

Take Action: The Nourishing Soil Meditation

Close your eyes and imagine you are a seed in the soil surrounded by rich moisture and yummy mineral nutrients. With every breath, receive those nutrients into your body and watch your roots and shoots start to grow. What does that feel like in your body? Describe your experience.

PLEASURE OR LOVE

When you let go of the hope of ever finding the unconditional nourishment and care you want in the people around you, you finally start your journey to true connection within. And it is the connection within that enables you to build true community in the world around you. You need to *embody* it in order to *create* it.

An important thing to remember is, that when talking about feeling unconditionally nourished and loved, this is not the same as feeling pleasure. Pleasure is a temporary experience and when you pursue it, you will have to constantly keep rearranging the world to find it. The world is unpredictable and so is your mind, and the things that give you pleasure today, may or may not be there tomorrow. And, as we discussed in the section on suicide Tuesday, even if they *are* there tomorrow, your mind may not get the same pleasure from them as it did the first time.

Most of us wander around mistaking pleasure for love at every turn. It can be difficult to give up looking for connection and love in the things that give you pleasure in life. In fact, it can be very depressing, which is why this process is called the dark night of the soul. Because you have to face how disappointing pleasure is and you have to face the *suicide Tuesday effect*.

When you stop trying to get love in the ways you have been taught, it can seem like you are giving up on ever having it, even though this, of course, is not the case. You are simply giving up the plastic for the gold - the temporary for the eternal. You are giving up a life of seeking approval by creating a false self for a life of creating genuine connection; by bringing love with you wherever you go, instead of seeking it wherever you go.

Journaling prompt:

How have you been mistaking pleasure, happiness, or 'feeling good' for unconditional love and nourishment sourced from within?

Take action:

What is one thing you can do right now, this second, that will help you connect to a source of love and nourishment within yourself? Take whatever comes to you, and give yourself that love and nourishment now.

THE ELUSIVE SEARCH FOR HOME

To have an innate knowledge of yourself and yet doubt yourself, can feel like being in a prison created by other people's ideas and imagined judgements. In that prison, it is the constant search for a true home that keeps you going. A constant belief that there is a place of safety, nourishment and love that is given to you unconditionally. You continue to search for this experience because you know it exists and can instinctively remember it - the experience of being in your mother's womb. In that womb you were fed, you were safe, and you were comfortable. On a deep, non-verbal plain of knowledge, you know it. You have been there. You have had a home - a paradise - and, being born, you were subsequently banished from it.

Most people in the West are familiar with the biblical story of the banishment from the Garden of Eden. Adam and Eve lived there happily with no worries whatsoever and then they were banished from it. Looking at this myth from the perspective of our physical body, you can see why it exists. The experience of being in paradise and then being banished from it is one we all come into this world having known. It is the experience of being connected to an umbilical cord in the womb and then being banished from the womb into an uncomfortable and dangerous surroundings.

In the biblical story, Adam and Eve 'sinned' and were punished by having to go live in a world where they were subject to the pains of birth and death and where they must work for their daily bread. This is the world we are born into. But not in every version of the story did Adam and Eve 'sin.' There are alternate versions of this story where the heroes choose to leave paradise on their own.

Do you remember what the 'sin' was that Adam and Eve were banished for? In the original story they were banished from their paradise because they ate from the forbidden fruit of The Tree of Knowledge of Good and Evil. In the alternate version, Adam and Eve decide to take a journey into duality and polarity. They had curiosity and were striving for knowledge and new experiences. They couldn't get that in paradise where nothing ever changes or challenges.

When living in paradise, there is a desire to gain knowledge through direct experience. In experiential embodied reality, you long for paradise. It's one of those 'the grass is always greener on the other side of the fence' type ironies. Unconsciously, you yearn to be back in paradise - at 'home' (which is essentially a feeling of safety, nourishment, and connection). But you live in a world of experience. One that you need to have a physical, mortal, and vulnerable body to appreciate.

But the experience of longing for that paradise-safety remains. And you look for it everywhere. In drugs, in food, in sex, in television, and in co-dependent relationships. You may find yourself stuck in your 'comfort zone' for this same reason, where you become comfortable and feel 'safe' in a situation even though it doesn't fulfill or express the real you, and where your true curiosity cannot be shared. The comfort zone is a distorted form of paradise because it feels safe, but in order to grow, you must be willing to express your curiosity and desire for something better. This will mean leaving paradise, working hard and truly experiencing life with its joys and pains to thrive as the authentic you.

The world we live in isn't safe, and even if you are living a lie or living in your comfort zone, something could happen to completely shake up your world. The true feeling of home can only be found through the internal connection to the source of nourishment and love you are building, because that is when you successfully bridge the gap between paradise and Earth. Between unity and connection and life in the form of duality.

Some say that our sole purpose for being born is to bridge that gap. To create a world where we have it all. To be mortal and yet aware of our own immortality and *connectivity* with a spiritual source. Whatever you believe about this being our purpose, the fact remains: you are here, you yearn to be *there* and, at least internally, it is possible to recreate that feeling. And externally? Externally you can help create a more collaborative world by radiating connection from within you wherever you go. You can help create a world that is fair, equitable and, if not safe from natural disasters, at least one where it is safe for us to be ourselves with each other.

There is another very important perspective on the Adam and Eve story to share. It is the perspective that as you grow up, you are ingrained with ideas of what good and evil are - conditioned by your parents and your environment. It is only when you start to understand your environment's concept of good vs. evil (once you take a bite off that apple of belief), that you are banished from paradise. It wasn't that eating the 'apple' was a sin, it was your understanding of the concept of good vs. evil that made you start to experience aspects of yourself as 'sinful'.

When you start to experience yourself as sinful, you are banished from your childhood innocence, and you start to form an alternative self. An alternative self based on feelings of shame, guilt, and regret. And you start to live in fear of consequences. When you start to see yourself as 'evil' (or just plain old bad) you start to close yourself off to the natural love and nourishment that live inside of you, and to close yourself off to innocence and paradise, because you no longer believe that you deserve them.

But when you realize that the love and nourishment you want are feelings you have already experienced before coming into this world and as a baby, it makes it much easier to find them again in the present. All you need do is remember that paradise does exist, do the Being in Connection practice, and receive it into yourself. In the next chapter on the pillar of receptivity, there will be much more information for you about how to better, well, *receive* this into yourself. And much more about overcoming shame and regret.

Action step: Back in the Womb Meditation

Close your eyes and take a few deep breaths. Imagine what it might be like to be back in the womb. Imagine the safety and the unconditional love and nourishment you receive there. The memory of that place exists within you, so invite that memory to the surface. The memory will be tactile, not verbal and not visual, so pay attention to your body's experience, not your mind's. Describe what you experienced in your journal.

A TRUE LEADER OF THE HEART

If your pillar of connection is weak, your internalized experience of isolation will come up again and again. This is good. It's coming up to be experienced and healed. It's not easy. In fact, it can be very painful. But your ability to be strong in the face of the recurring pain will return you to innocence and your true interconnection with all that is will reawaken. Building your pillar of vision gives you the power to face the pain, and facing your pain, strengthens your vision. It's an upward spiral.

If the task of building your pillar of connection isn't clear yet, that's normal. Continue reading about the pillars of receptivity and creativity and things will start to fall into place. The pillars are also a spiral staircase and you will need to gradually build all of them in order to build up any single one. Meanwhile, you can think of building your pillar of connection as a three step process. The Present, The Past, and The Future.

Step one: The Present

Build the experience of love and nourishment within you in the present.

Utilize the Forgiveness Ritual in the appendix and practice the Being in Connection meditation described above to help heal the isolation within you and build an experience of connection in present time. You can ask whatever or whoever you find at the other end of the umbilical cord how to move forward in your life, and how you can help create a creative, reciprocal environment for yourself to live in. You can also utilize the journaling prompts and action steps in this chapter alongside the Pillar Practices appendix for more ideas. In addition, on the website you will find a special meditation for conscious relationship which can be used to build the connection with your internal *beloved*, as Rumi would call it. As Jungian psychology describes it: your anima/animus (your inner masculine/feminine counter-balance to your physical gender).

Without practicing, you will not make changes in the unconscious mind, which is the beginning of healing. This cannot be emphasized enough. Without doing the practices and building a new experience for yourself in the present, the new ways in which you will be asked to rise up and make your voice heard may continue to be impossible to surmount.

Step two: The Past

Identify the places in your past that get triggered and create the fear of isolation.
Remember, if you fear isolation, it is because you have experienced it before and that experience has not been fully processed. The task of healing the experience of isolation is a long one. But it's not one where you need to confront and heal every past experience of isolation. Rather, the major task is to teach yourself how to feel connected, loved and nourished in the present. That said, it helps to put a face on your past isolation experiences to lessen their control over you. To start accessing those past experiences, you can use your present day fear of isolation as a peephole into the past. You can do that with the following exercise:

Make a table with three columns.
1. **First column header: In my current environment, who do I fear will try and make me feel isolated if I authentically express myself?** Answering this question gives you a glimpse of the feeling of isolation that currently lives inside of you and controls you. You open this up so you can utilize it as a window (or peephole) to gaze into your past.

2. **Second column header: Write down the name of a person that caused you to feel isolated in the past that the person in column one reminds you of. Or that caused a similar kind of isolation feeling.** Doing this allows you to see where the original experience of isolation might be. Admittedly, this is a tricky thing to discern. A feeling of isolation can be something you experienced as a child and unconsciously internalized. Something as simple as not being comforted as you cried yourself to sleep in your crib. Whatever comes to mind, though, write it down. Don't censor yourself.

   Note: You may find that you have a hard time finding a past experience that is equivalent to the feeling of isolation you fear in the present. Try doing the Being in Connection practice and asking your source of nourishment on the other side of the umbilical cord to help you see. You will gain more tools for this kind of work in the next chapter.

3. **Third column header: What is the wisdom I gained from the experience of isolation I had?** No matter how painful the experience was, there is wisdom to pull from it. Even if it's as simple as, 'Never let a child cry themselves to sleep, even though the culture may say it is ok to do so.' Or, 'Always be compassionate to children.' Every negative experience is a source of wisdom. Finding that wisdom will help you start turning your pain into compost that nourishes your future gardens. And it will strengthen your pillar of vision as well.

You can download a template with these columns on the author's website.

Step three: The Future

Express yourself in a new and collaborative way.

In any of your life situations, you can use your ability as an empath to become a community builder. The first challenge you will face in that process is to clearly translate into words what you intuitively feel is going on in other people's hearts and minds. You will need to find words that express to them what you see and know in a compassionate and collaborative (as opposed to an aggressive or accusatory) way.

The second challenge is to rise up and find the courage to actually express it. Utilizing steps one and two (The Present and The Past) and your pillar of vision will help you find the courage. To face the first challenge of expressing yourself, try the following journaling exercise:

Make a table with 2 columns.

1. **Column one header: In what current day situations do I keep my voice hidden?** This can be a work or personal situation but it can also be when you have a creative idea for yourself and the voices in your head put it down.

3. **Column two header: How can I create a more comfortable and safer environment for myself in this situation?** Do you need to have a one-on-one or mediated conversation with somebody? Do you need to ask a group you work with to listen to you without interruption or to give you more space to express yourself? Do you need to ask your marriage partner to go to counseling with you? Do you need to meditate more? Do you need to sit on the couch and breath? Any ideas are welcome, no matter how small or out of the box they are.

To complete this exercise, you will take action on your second column insights. The action phase can be broken down into three components: **Reinvent the Feeling, Rehearse the Words, and Remember the Goal.**

Reinvent the Feeling

How do you want to reinvent your environments and relationships? First, decide on a 'reinvention goal' and write it down. For example: 'My goal for reinventing my workplace is to help create an environment where everybody's voice is respected, and everybody feels safe to communicate authentically about all levels of their being.' When you have a goal in mind, find the feeling of that goal in your body.

To find the feeling, sit with the words you wrote, close your eyes and feel the outcome that you desire. Ask yourself, 'When I think about having achieved my outcome, how does my body feel?' Remember this feeling. You can bring your attention back to it again and again as needed. Knowing that as you feel that outcome, you are more likely to make choices that will lead you to it. You can even choose a small object that will remind you of that desired outcome and carry it with you.

One thing to be aware of is to make sure you are not creating your reinvention goal by projecting the unconscious desire for the feeling of paradise. The biggest disappointments lay in this direction. Remember that any goal (or vision) you have for a change in your environment will forever be something that you adapt. You will never be able to create circumstances outside yourself that will create the feeling of paradise. Paradise only exists within you.

You can experience relief, joy, contentment, freedom, and similar positive emotions, but none of these are long lasting. It is good to create them in your life, of course, just never expect them to be eternal. The feeling of eternal paradise can only be found within you by building the pillar of connection. It lives in a place completely apart from any external conditions.

So, when you are setting your goal for reinventing your life, expect positive change, and expect positive emotion to follow, but realize it will never be perfect, and you will always be on a journey of learning and growth. In the next chapter on receptivity, you will learn more about building paradise within you and letting go of the need for perfection.

Take action:

Write down at least 2 reinvention goals you have. Remember to include the changes in feeling as well as the environmental changes you wish to see.

Rehearse the Words

You start the process by feeling the potential that a more conscious environment can create (this is your reinvention goal as discussed above). Next, you need to rehearse the words. Do this by writing down your insights into the situation and the people involved ahead of time and then going over what you want to say. Go over it again and again and again so that you don't lose yourself when you are in the moment.

When you are rehearsing, trust your intuition about what the other person is going through and write down ways to ask them if what you perceive is true. When you are planning how to ask about it, use phrases that don't contain absolutes. Words such as 'may,' 'maybe,' and 'might' could be utilized. For example: 'It seems to me that you might be experiencing… (exhaustion, fear of failure, anger about…) is that true?'

Also use validation when you speak. For example: 'I see your points about _____ (here actually reflect back to them what you heard them say) and I want to add to these points you made by sharing my own perspectives. Are you willing to listen until I'm done before responding?' When you are reflecting what you understood they were saying, expect that they may interrupt and want to correct you if you misunderstood.

If anybody is disrespectful to you in this process, you can ask them for the same courtesies that you are offering:

1. Not to make assumptions about what you are going through but rather to ask if what they think is correct.

2. To reflect back to you what they heard you say and for you to be able to correct them over and over again until they get it right.

In addition to not using absolutes and using validation and reflection, you can use the examples given above in the section titled, 'Sample Conversations' to rehearse the words you are going to use.

Remember the Goal

People may deny that your insights are true or argue with you. That's all okay. When this kind of conflict comes up (and it will), remember that your goal as an empathic community builder is to create a more community oriented and supportive environment. The purpose of the conversation is to open a door, not to be acknowledged for being right and not to create paradise (an eternal feeling of safety and peace).

When conflict arises, you will need to stretch yourself to be vulnerable, curious, and authentic, especially in situations where you might be making changes to long standing agreements or ways of relating. So, when you feel like defending yourself or surrendering your own voice, bring your attention back to the feeling of your goal in your body. *Remember* it.

Hold to the physical feeling of the potential outcome you have already imagined. Allow that feeling to guide you and the conversation to the fulfillment of that goal. It will take practice and courage to change any deeply ingrained habits of hiding and to become an empathic community builder. And it may take more than one conversation. It may take months or even years. But all you need do is hold the feeling of the potential for positive, collaborative outcome in your body and let it lead you to your goal. No matter how long it takes.

To sum up these action steps:

1. **Reinvent**: Hold to the feeling and vision of a collaboration and allow it to guide you and pull you forward. Don't expect paradise, expect imperfect progress.

2. **Rehearse:** Think about what you want to say and how you want to say it before you enter into the conversations.

3. **Remember:** When you get sucked into an argument, or feel the need to hide your voice, take a pause, remember the feeling of your goal, and let that feeling move you forward again.

If you are afraid of a severe response, create a safety net for yourself. Making sure you have somebody to turn to for help if you need it.

In sum, just like the pillars of intuition themselves, these three steps for building the pillar of connection (past, present, and future) are a process and a spiral staircase. Deepen your internal experience of connection in the present, take a step towards healing past wounds, and then take some action to create a better future (even if in a small way).

Then go back to step one and continue to elevate your experience of internal love and nourishment in the present, creating an upward spiral motion.

Take action for the present:

Choose 1 practice for building connection from this chapter or from the appendix and do it now.

Journaling prompt for the past:

Do the Wisdom Gathering exercise from the second step (The Past).

Journaling prompt for the future:

Do the Comfortable Environments exercise from step three (The Future). In addition to the 2 column table, pick one situation that you want to bring change to. Set yourself up for action by reinventing the feeling of the outcome (creating a clear goal) and rehearsing the words you might use in the conversation.

CHANGE

Sometimes, even if you build love within yourself, learn to express your thoughts authentically, and strive for true connection with your environment, it doesn't work. They don't reciprocate. If over and over again, the people in your environment won't grow and learn with you, then you may need a better environment. You can't spend your life trying to change other people and make them more collaborative and creative. You have a creative genius and you deserve an environment and community that supports it.

You are an equal. To build your pillar of connection, be curious, project a spirit of collaboration and connection from within yourself and communicate effectively so that your environment knows better how to interact with you. The most important component of these is to cultivate a deep feeling of connection within yourself in the present. When you have that feeling, that's when courage overcomes fear, and all the rest flows naturally.

You may have been telling yourself to hide in certain situations. That's no longer necessary. When you build your pillar of connection, you become a genuine genius at being with people. You become a leader of the heart with empathic rare intelligence and you make the world a better place by fully expressing that.

Journaling Prompt:

Who are the people you know or have met that you believe have a strong pillar of connection. What can you learn from them?

Take action:

Ask the people you know who have a strong pillar of connection for advice on building yours. Reach out to at least one person right now. Journal about the advice they give.

BUILDING THE PILLAR OF RECEPTIVITY

THE PILLAR

A life lacking in receptivity is a life where you think you have to do everything on your own. Where you are not able to receive the support you need, or you do not believe such support exists. A life where you lack the time and energy for the things you love and the people you love the most. Before building your pillar of receptivity, you might find yourself drowning in your own life and gasping for air. Your inner voice shut away, deep in the far recesses of your mind, begging for attention.

In contrast, if you have already built your pillar of receptivity, you will find you are able to live *in-between the moments*, completely in sync with the universal clock and connected to the deep spacious and timeless nature of the universe. In-between the moments, there is no concern for how long something will take; you always know that the timing is perfect, and you trust that everything arrives when you are in need of it.

You know this because you are receptive to the non-verbal, mystical essence that permeates the universe. What in Sanskrit is called Sat-Chit-Ananda - The Blissful Intelligence of the Universe or in China, The Eternal Tao. In Western New-Age terms, you would talk about trusting Life or The Universe. When you receive support from The Blissful Intelligence of the Universe, you are able to use your intuition as a guidance system to navigate your life and achieve your goals.

The ancient Chinese master Lao Tzu, author of the Tao De Jing is somebody who exemplified receptivity. So is Saint Hildegard of Bingen, a twelfth century nun who accomplished an incredible amount in her life, all while maintaining her mystical connection and ability to enter into visionary, mystical states. And in your own life? Think about that friend who always seems to be taking risks and trusting that everything will work out. And it does! Think about the successful entrepreneurs who take regular breaks for meditation to restore their vigor. They too are successfully living in receptivity.

And you yourself? Perhaps you too have a story to tell about how you followed your inner voice on a whim and ended up on a crazy adventure. A time when you listened deeply to the intelligence of life and when you had the clarity of mind to know when to say yes, and when to say no, when to turn left, and when to turn right, no matter what the logical mind said and no matter what fears came up on that journey.

When you build the pillar of receptivity and your ability to listen deeply to the spaciousness within you, you will always find balance. Balance of time for yourself, and time for others. Time for chores, and time for indulgence. Time for practical work, and time for meditation. And when your boundaries get pushed and the chores seem to pile up, you always rise to the challenge and stretch yourself yet again so that the spaciousness in-between the moments lasts even longer and everything gets done in perfect timing and in balance with your need to rest and receive.

Journaling prompt:

Have you had times in your life when you have felt this kind of 'flow'? A time when you could tune into something greater than yourself and *know* you are supported and guided by something greater? Close your eyes and reconnect with what those moments were like. Describe the feeling and experience.

THE CHALLENGE: TIME IS NOT THE ENEMY

You deserve to love yourself, but if you are still building your pillar of receptivity, it's probably been a while since you spent quality time enjoying your own company. It's understandable, though, between all the tasks required of you, it can be hard to find the time to live in balance. And yet you probably want to model spaciousness and balance for those you love and for the world around you. If you can't model it, you can't offer it to others, and you can't create the world as you wish it to be.

Time, however, is only the apparent enemy. There is something much deeper going on at the emotional and mental levels when you are unable to be receptive to what you need and your relationship with your inner voice is out of harmony. There is a reason why one person looks at the calendar and sees free time and rejoices, and another looks at the same calendar and starts to panic.

Each one of these people has an underlying inner dialogue that is guiding their view of the world. When you look at the calendar (or somebody asks you to do something) and it makes you want to run and hide in your closet, it's a sign you are unconsciously carrying a fear of being out of control. It prevents your tremendous creative abilities from fully manifesting in *co-creation* with the vast intelligence of the universe.

It's easy to fall prey to a need to feel in control as we are often taught that to feel worthy, we need to be 'Type-A' superheroes that accomplish everything on their own. Over-stimulation and busyness is an epidemic in our society and many people measure their worth by how many activities they partake in instead of how connected they are to the truth within themselves. If you are constantly trying to prove your worth by saying yes to too many things, you could be unconsciously sabotaging your inner voice. Because to receive the light that comes from within, you must feel worthy of it.

AVOIDING REST

When you feel like you need to accomplish so much that you just don't have the time, your life becomes a race, and when racing becomes a long-term habit, it becomes increasingly difficult to rest, even when you want to rest and mange to find the time. If your ability to receive is off line, you may find you have worked your body and mind into such a state of fatigue that if you sit down to rest, weariness will simply take over. But the opposite can be true as well.

You have probably experienced this at some point in your life: you try to take a short rest but a nagging fear kicks in – a fear that you won't take care of all your responsibilities. A fear that the people who depend on you will be disappointed. A fear that if you slow down to rest that a tsunami will drown everything in your life and the volcano erupting within you will spill over and burn everything in sight.

One irony in this situation is that this can actually lead you to avoid resting – and it's a downward spiral from there because it is in those short rest breaks throughout the day that you can become receptive and your inner voice can speak to you. Those moments of stepping into a place of timelessness (even for just a second) are the moments that give you vitality, inspiration and energy to do all that you need to, and likely with a lot less mental and physical effort.

Depending on how long it's been since you had a strong pillar of receptivity, you may be so conditioned not to rest that your body has forgotten how to do it properly. You may be experiencing this state to such an extreme that slowing down is the most frightening thing in the world for you – triggering that fear of losing control. Hopefully, your life isn't this extreme, however, if not being able to receive support is an issue for you, then at some point, you have probably experienced having trouble with rest in this way.

Journaling prompt:

Where in your life do you find yourself trying to control things that may not need your control (emphasis on 'may')? In other words, what circumstances in your life trigger a desire to be in control (whether you consider that desire justified or not)? Consider the little things in life too. Things in your relationships, your home, your work, and anywhere else. Write down at least 5 places you feel the need to be in control.

Take action:

Pick one or two of these circumstances and next time you find yourself with a need to be in control in those circumstances, ask yourself what would happen if you trusted the flow of things. If instead of controlling, you chose to receive input and support from others. Circle the ones you have chosen.

A MUTUAL DANCE - PARTNERING WITH CHAOS

How would it feel if you were dancing with a partner who constantly tried to control the dance? If you are unable to be receptive, then that is what you are doing with the vast creative nature within you. How would it feel if you sat in an art class and the instructor stood over your shoulder telling you exactly which lines to draw? You would start feeling like a robot. Your spirit would slowly wither and hide. And yet this is what your conscious mind does to your inner voice when it takes over control.

And here's the bottom line – no matter how hard it tries, your conscious mind can never be completely in control. And the fact is, life is healthier and a lot more exciting when you don't try to control everything because the full spectrum of your consciousness has a chance to support you. Hijacking all your action with your conscious mind, leaves no room for intuition to come through, for creativity to blossom, and for chaos to create art in your life. It leaves no room for the mutual dance between you and all creation.

Hopefully, any desire you have to be in full control hasn't put you at the end of your rope, about to burn and crash from a lack of rest and an overdose of coffee (or worse). Hopefully, if you have an over-abundance of commitments and lack of receptivity in your life, it is only a trend. And hopefully, that trend will be easy to pull back from before it becomes a real disaster.

The best part? The solution doesn't involve trying to make time in your schedule for rest! At least not in the way that you might normally think of it. To build your pillar of receptivity, there is no need for you to take long walks in nature, meditate for 2 hours a day, take naps, or get a nanny (not that it wouldn't be great... just not necessary). Remember? It's not about having (or not having) time. It's really a fear of losing control and not being perfect (not living up to your internalized expectations of yourself) that closes the door on your ability to receive.

And the reason you may have this fear of losing control? It's because when your pillar of receptivity is not in place, a part of you really does feel out of control. That part of you is constantly chasing an image of what you are supposed to be, but it can never quite seem to attain it. You might feel like you are constantly trying to catch-up with something and never doing enough. The solution is building your ability to be receptive and accepting that you deserve support even though you are imperfect.

You accomplish this by first building your connection to a source of love and nourishment within you. And to whatever degree, you have already done that! The next step is enhancing your ability to receive that love and nourishment by stepping into the spaciousness and timelessness that exists *in-between the moments* - even for just a few seconds at a time. And you need to learn to do this even though it feels like stepping into that timelessness will bring chaos to the false order your mind has tried to create. You need to let that false order come crashing down and be willing to sit with the uncomfortable feelings it will produce, at least initially.

When you enter a spacious, timeless, and receptive state, you tune into a higher genius and find that creative and out-of-the-box ideas and perspectives are simply handed to you. You learn to receive the love and nourishment you need to courageously follow your inner voice. The irony, once again, is that you may blame time limitations for holding you back. But in reality, it's not taking a few seconds here and there to be receptive to a timeless source of inspiration within you that causes all the stress.

If this situation is bad for you, what you may not realize is that if you don't become more receptive to support, life will fly by in a panicked blur. And that it really will be the end of *your* world (and body) before you know it. If you want to make a real and positive impact on the world and the people you love, you will need to realize that it's better to be present than to be perfect. It's hard to have a relationship with somebody who's never there.

When you build the pillar of receptivity all your relationships and activities fall into place because it is only in co-creation with your inner voice that you can really create the kind of harmony you are looking for. The reactive mind can't do it. You need to learn to take those moments of inspired rest throughout your day and in those moments, be willing to receive the love and nourishment you need.

The conscious mind is limited and isn't meant to be as active as we have made it in the modern era. Think about our ancestors – living tribal lives close to nature. They walked everywhere and were acutely aware of their environment. As they walked, they would read messages on the ground, their senses naturally attuned to discern where food might be or animals might be hiding. They lived the mystery of it, and had plenty of time to be curious and be in-between the moments - processing, balancing, observing, integrating, imagining, and receiving inspiration from beyond. It is only in that kind of mindset that intuitions can come through.

Journaling prompts:
1. Do you deserve support even though you are imperfect?
2. Is there a part of you that feels it's not doing enough? If so, unconsciously, who is that part of you trying to please or impress?
3. Who do you want to 'be there for' in your life (that perhaps you don't spend enough time with)?

Take action: Timelessness Meditation

Close your eyes and slip into an in-between moment, inviting a sense of timelessness (whatever your current understanding of that may be). Observe your mind and notice two things: First, how difficult is it for you to enter that state? Second, when you try and enter it, what emotions and fears turn up in your mind? Describe your experience.

SHAME AND REGRET

If you have a problem receiving support, it is probably because you don't feel worthy of it. It is the gap between who you are and who you think you should be that creates that feeling of unworthiness. Because who would feel worthy if no matter how hard they tried, they were never actually able to keep up with everything? And even when they did manage to accomplish something, the results just never seemed to be up to par.

If you have difficulty receiving and you carry any feelings of unworthiness, then shame and regret were probably taught to you as a child when you were disciplined through the culture of punishment and maybe even humiliation. A culture where you were regularly compared to others (either in real life or on television) and forced to compete. The message was that the gift of a fulfilling life is only available through the validation of people in authority. It is this kind of education that often leads to an unconscious sense of powerlessness and a feeling of being 'out of control,' in which you just can't thrive.

Another way to look at being 'out of control' or powerless is that you are unconsciously *under* the control of others, be it your parents, Disney, or the pecking order on the playground. From the moment you were born, people have been teaching you to be the way they want you to be. They taught you that to receive their support you first must appease their will. It is also possible that you were taught that in order to get praise and attention you had to be perfect and you were never given the message that you can celebrate being human in all your flaws or that you can simply be happy celebrating your strengths and natural talents. It is having been imperfect in your accomplishments, made mistakes, and/or hurt people out of ignorance, that creates regret.

Shame was created by people's negative reactions to your imperfections and it may still be alive in you today as an ingrained voice in your unconscious mind. These are negative unconscious reactions to yourself that rather than creating cooperation and growth, re-create the experience of punishment and the withdrawal of love. They may even create an unconscious perception that no matter what you do, you are not worthy of support, creating the desire to constantly take on more and more responsibility and do it all on your own in order to prove your worth.

When you try to be in control, more and more, the in-between moments slip away from you because it is exactly the ability to be in co-control (or co-creation) with The

Blissful Intelligence of the Universe (and with other people) that allows spaciousness and timelessness to enter your life. Spaciousness and timelessness allow you to return to your original state of innocence and receptivity. They are what allow you to have little restful moments throughout the day where you can find inspiration and connect to your intuition.

You may never have been given the message that life is a process. That no one does anything without making mistakes and real accomplishments take time and plenty of trial and error before you succeed (and that even then, it won't be 'perfect'). It's true of every master creator that you ask, that they are never content with their 'masterpieces'. In interview after interview accomplished people always say that they could have done more or that they obsess over the little flaws in their work that no one else can see.

It's completely natural to strive for perfection, but it is insanity to allow that striving to prevent you from feeling accomplished or from even receiving the knowledge and support you need to begin creating. Your entire life you will inevitably make mistakes and hurt people as you learn about yourself, your art, and others. Creation is a process of ever improving yourself. And the only way to improve is to take action and then see how the world responds. It is a feedback loop, without which you cannot accomplish your vision.

If you had received honest feedback and supportive encouragement instead of punishment and shaming when you made mistakes, you would have learned to master co-creation. You would know that you can't accomplish anything without first stepping on some toes and making a mess of things. You would know that you can't create anything without the feedback of others who help you make it better, and that this feedback loop is an upward spiral of co-creation.

But if you are afraid of that feedback loop causing shame or regret, you will never even start down the road of creating your vision. You will continue striving to be validated, exhausting yourself again and again along the way. Getting rid of shame and regret is not the goal, however, as they will continue to appear both as memories and as a result of new mistakes you make. When they appear, it will be up to you what you do with them. You can make them into logs that you beat yourself down with or into logs that fuel the fire of your determination, igniting compassion and action.

No matter how many times you make the same mistake, or how many times you don't take an action that you know would make you proud of yourself, or how many times you hide away and don't give yourself a chance to make the difficult and uncomfortable choice you know is the right one… you must throw the logs of regret and shame into the fire. Make them fuel your determination and compassion (for yourself and for others suffering in the same way). And each time you do, know that you get closer to lifting yourself up into being the person you know you can be.

Without dealing with shame and regret and the internalized stories about being unworthy, you cannot rise to fully receive what you deserve. You will always encounter unconscious self-sabotaging thoughts and fatigue instead. And the truly terrible thing about this is that it's not just you. Most people who were brought up in the culture of punishment carry this type of shame and regret as well.

If this all sounds too familiar, there are some very easy-to-apply solutions to help you build your pillar of receptivity and restore your faith in your inner voice. The best part is… they won't take any extra time to implement! You can do them in-between the moments… And you will learn exactly how to attain those in-between moments further down.

Journaling prompts:
1. What have you accomplished in your life (no matter how imperfect those accomplishments were)? Make a list of at least 5-10 things you feel proud of.
2. What do you feel shame and regret about (make a list of 5-10 things)?
3. How can you use the shame and regret you feel to fuel your vision and compassion?
4. Describe the gap between who you are and the person you think you should already be.
5. Who has you under their control - both as an imprint in your mind, and in your present life?
6. Are there times when you feel like you have to do it all on your own in order to prove your worth? What are those times?

Take action:

Celebrate being human in all your flaws. Take yourself out to dinner and for a walk in the park. Maybe invite your friends over to dance and have a 'being a flawed human' party. Maybe create a ceremony for yourself. It's up to you how you celebrate. Through this celebration, give yourself permission to be your authentic self.

YOU DESIRE A FEELING

All of your actions are guided by your underlying desire to feel good and how you can achieve those desired feelings. You may make the mistake of thinking that you desire an object or outcome outside yourself. But in truth, you desire a feeling or state of mind, and you associate that feeling with the attainment of objects or outcomes in your life. When you are looking into your desired outcomes, look at the feelings you are trying to bring into your life through those desires. The feelings are what you truly desire, and the choices you make in your life are all attempts to live in those feelings regularly.

For example: You might have a desire to attain a certain benchmark in your career, or maybe you have a desire for true love. But what do you imagine that a love relationship will bring you? Or hitting that benchmark? A closer look will most likely reveal that what you truly desire is that feeling of 'home' - of safety, validation, acceptance, nourishment, and unconditional love. In other words, in both these cases, you are most likely trying to recreate the emotional state of 'paradise,' that we all seek to return to.

Unconsciously, it is often this feeling of paradise that is the imagined outcome of the things you want to achieve or have in your life. It is ironic, however, because the feeling of paradise is the experience of knowing that you don't have to do or be anything except yourself to feel connected and supported - it is not something that comes from attainment. The opposite is true, it is feeling inwardly nourished, and connected that enables us to attain anything real and lasting.

It is this innate and universal desire for connection that is why you build your pillars of vision and receptivity. Building your pillar of vision gives you the drive you need to overcome your unconscious resistance to receiving, and it is receptivity that allows you to enter into connection with your inner voice. Finally, it is your pillar of connection that allows you to feel safe enough to open your heart to the silence within you, and that silence is what allows creativity to naturally overflow. When you are in that perfect creative flow, you live in the experience of fulfilling your purpose in life.

Understanding your underlying desire for paradise calls into question your need to attain your existing goals, or bring those objects and relationships you desire into your life. It calls into question whether those things are really what will make you happy in life. And calling all this into question is an important step towards freedom.

There is nothing wrong with desires and goals, so long as your goals flow from the silence of your heart and not from your conditioned mind. But what if after a deep examination of yourself you determine that there *is* something you desire to attain that is for yourself, and not for the approval of others? That it is truly something that comes from the silence in your heart? A restful, in-between the moments, co-creative, look at this goal will probably reveal that there is a better way of moving yourself towards that goal than what you are doing now.

When you do find a desire or goal that flows organically from the silence in your heart it is a profound experience. It is one of beginning to understand your true purpose in life. Your ability to hold that goal in mind and communicate it to your inner voice in those in-between moments will bring you the information and inspiration you need to move yourself forward, not because of some kind of 'manifestation magic,' but because you will make better choices for yourself based on your intuition, and guided by your inner voice. You will learn how to do this in detail further into this chapter.

When you are striving to accomplish something in your life or to simply get through your to-do list for the day and you hit a wall, it is a sign you are craving connection. It is a sign that you need to look for a restful in-between moment where you can receive support from something greater than yourself. A moment where you can allow love and nourishment to pour into you so that intuition and inspiration can guide you. It is only there, in that in-between moment, that you can receive the knowledge you need to move yourself forward more sustainably.

It is not in pushing for the attainment of your goals that you find rest. It is in rest, that you find the path to the attainment of your goals. Nothing outside yourself can provide the feeling of paradise. Once you formulate the feeling of paradise within yourself by building your pillar of connection, you stop trying to attain the impossible. You stop trying to attain paradise from objects or attainments in the imperfect external world. When you establish that feeling of paradise within yourself, you become free to pursue the true goals and desires that come from the silence in your heart.

We will talk more about finding the silence in your heart in the next chapter on creativity. For now, become aware of your underlying desire for the feeling of 'paradise.' Start to understand what the feeling of paradise really is and how focusing on it, already starts to transform your body.

Take action: Feeling at Home Meditation

Close your eyes, and sink into the feeling of paradise. Of being 'at home'. Being safe, cared for, loved and nourished (whatever you imagine that to be like). Observe how that feeling starts to change things in your mind and body. Also observe the mental resistance you might have to that feeling. You will know you are in resistance if your body and breath start to contract. Journal about your experience.

Journaling prompts:

Looking at the vision and goals you already created for yourself when building the pillar of vision:

1. What are the goals you have that you know don't come from the silence in your heart?

2. Which are the goals and desires that you feel come from the silent place within you?

BEING IN RELATIONSHIP WITH WHAT YOU WANT

When you see something you want, the tendency is to run and cling to it. When you recall a feeling you want to have (or imagine what a certain feeling might be like), your mind runs to it and attempts to cling to it too. But what happens when you chase after your desire? At some point in the chase, you hit a wall. You can also think of it as hitting a store window, where what you want is just beyond the glass. You end up with your nose pressed against the glass and a feeling of yearning or longing. The experience is that what you want to attain is just beyond reach.

When you run towards your desire, you hit a glass wall. You find that you can't immediately change who and how you are right now simply by desiring to be somewhere or something else. It's a mistake we all make. So what's the secret? The secret to getting the feeling you want is to be receptive and *in relationship* with what you want, instead of the idea that you lack it and have to perform a certain way in order to have it.

Instead of longing, be still, enter an in-between moment, and invite what you want to you, and then slowly develop a relationship with how it feels. If you want love, you need to develop a relationship with the feeling of love. You need to stop making assumptions that because you can imagine what love is, that you have any idea about what it actually is. Love isn't paradise. You need to take love out on a first date. Wine it and dine it. Get to know it. Be open minded to what getting to know it will mean to you and how it will change you, as any experience and relationship inevitably does.

If you see somebody you find attractive laying on the beach you can't go over to them and assume they will match up with your expectations. Though it's the approach most people unconsciously take. They try and 'get what they want' from the other person. This is the approach - you go up to that gorgeous person laying half naked on the beach and say, 'So… my ideal partner does the dishes every day, likes to dance, and makes me feel really good about myself. How about it?'

Needless to say, it's an approach that doesn't work very well. So instead, if you see somebody you are attracted to, you might go over with an open mind and no preconceptions. Be willing to receive who they actually are with genuine curiosity rather than expecting them to provide you with what you desire. Be accommodating, flexible, and humble, and be willing to upgrade yourself according to what you learn from them, and the relationship itself.

The principle is the same with all the feelings, objects, and attainments you desire. You must really get to know what you want and be willing to learn how it's going to change you when it comes. No experience you imagine having comes without a price: the growth and change you must experience in order to attain it. Internal growth in terms of how you understand the world and how you think, and external change in terms of how you act and the choices you make. If you don't embrace the changes you need to make in yourself, you will unconsciously reject what you want and sabotage yourself.

When you try and find a feeling you want outside yourself through achievements, relationships and objects, that's when you hit the glass wall. That glass represents the boundaries of your 'self.' You can't leave yourself to get what you want. You must stay grounded in your body while inviting what you want into it, and you have to make room for it and treat it with respect once you have it. You make room for it by clearing out old ideas and conditions about it.

If it's love you seek (or freedom or safety or anything else) you have to become aware of the in-between moments and then invite love to dance in that moment with you (and not be in total control of the dance). As you dance with love, you will become more acquainted with the truth of it and shed your illusions about it. If you decide to take the next step, you will have to make room for it inside yourself. Start by getting rid of some old clothes (old ideas) to make room for love to move in. Get comfortable with love's toothbrush next to yours in the bathroom and love hanging up a couple of suits in your closet for those cozy nights when it sleeps over. Most importantly, though, get comfortable with the mess it makes in your kitchen sometimes.

You may have expectations about what love will provide you with but anything you invite into yourself will inevitably offer you a few surprises. For example, you might find that as you build a relationship with love within you, that you end up broken hearted at the ending of a romantic relationship you thought was full of love. Perhaps because you needed to grow and shed your ideas about love in order to experience the truth of it. When you follow your inner voice and invite in what you want, you usually won't get exactly what you expected. But you will always get the truth. And that's a lot better.

In sum, when you want something (especially a feeling), the tendency is to chase after it. Naturally, you hit your head on the glass wall of your own outer shell. Instead of chasing, learn to build a relationship with what you want and invite it into your home and into your body. Keep in mind the fact that you may not be used to sharing your home in this way and that you will have to change and grow to accommodate it.

Journaling prompts:

1. On a scale of 1-10 (1 being weakest) how willing are you to make changes in the way you think about what you want?

2. What changes are you willing to make to the ways you think about what you want?

3. On a scale of 1-10 (1 being weakest), how willing are you to start turning to the in-between moments to find inspiration instead of thinking you can do it all yourself?

4. How are you going to implement turning to the in-between moments for inspiration instead of trying to do it all yourself?

5. How will you motivate yourself to truly make these changes?

Take action: Being the Change Meditation

Recall the feeling of something you want being just beyond reach. Now make a mental shift to be *in relationship* with that object, feeling or attainment. Start allowing that relationship to change you so that what you want can move in. Imagine yourself emptying some drawers to make room for it. Write about your experience and how you will apply this same principle to your future desires.

CONTEMPLATE THIS

To help you ease your need for control and allow your inner voice space to re-ignite a natural and easy flow in your life, you can contemplate the following:

1. **The Feeling:** Remember that it is a feeling you are chasing and that a feeling is created by your perspective on the world. When you perceive you have done well, you feel proud. When you feel proud, you can rest. Your job is done.

2. **Change:** Realize that constantly trying to rearrange the world to make yourself feel a certain way is an endless and pointless endeavor. The world is always changing so as soon as you arrange it in one way and shift your attention, something changes and you have to go back and make it all 'perfect' again. Be in relationship with the feeling you want rather than trying to create the circumstances you think will create it.

3. **Focus:** Even though there are things you might not have done well, there are also plenty of things you have done well. What you focus on - grows (this isn't magic, it's simply a matter of creating and re-enforcing these patterns in your mind). Practice noticing everything you are doing right. Highlight and celebrate even the smallest of things like brushing your teeth, texting someone you have been meaning to respond to, or feeding your body healthy food.

4. **Chaos:** Chaos will always cause the wind to blow the leaves off the trees and mess up the yard you just cleaned. Making friends with chaos is a must as it is the sense of humor of the universe. It is your reminder to be humble and grateful. Without these little jabs, you would think you were the greatest thing since the invention of push notifications from your calendar app. It is in the humble realization of your smallness that true freedom is born.

5. **Perfection:** Surrender to the dance of life. 'Process over schedule' is a motto you might adopt. People are more important than accomplishments. Patience and love are more important than making yourself or anybody else try to achieve a nonsensical image of perfection. There are many things in life that are not under your control. That's actually a good thing – it means you are responsible for far less than you think!

Journaling prompt:
Choose one of these 5 and write about how you can apply that principle to your life.

RECEIVING FROM THE INNER VOICE

You can't change your mental patterns. Change happens, yes, but 'you' can't create that change. Trying to change your own mental patterns is like asking a rock to sculpt itself. The rock requires an artist. That artist is your inner voice.

You know what the great sculptors always say? They say that they simply uncover the beauty that is inside the rock - they are not creating, they are unveiling. So call out to the artist within you and invite it to sculpt you! What you have been trying to do is sculpt yourself, to somehow reach outside yourself with your insights into your true nature and chisel away. It doesn't work very well.

There is a force beyond your own conscious mind that is the only force that can help you change. Your only task is to receive it. No path to fully embodying your inner wisdom will be quicker than getting the pipe cleaner out and clearing the receptivity channels; by clearing away the perfectionism, fears, and self-sabotaging beliefs. It allows your inner voice to pour its energy into you, and re-shape your life from the inside out.

The question is - are you fully on board to be your authentic self? Even if your conscious mind says yes, there is likely a part of your mind that's not on board yet. The part of your mind that stores your unconscious stories and beliefs about yourself and life. Those unconscious beliefs block you from being who you want to be, and create those really bothersome patterns we're all desperate to get rid of.

Think of it as a small child (your unconscious) holding up a wall (your resistance) that is holding back a tidal wave (your desire to be your true self). That is how much energy is wasted trying to hold an image of yourself and of life that is not true. This is why some people walk around so incredibly tired and depressed. Think of all the good that energy could do in the world!

The more you learn to consciously receive from the inner voice shaping you and melt through your unconscious resistance, the quicker you will embody your insights and live as the person you actually are. There are many specific unconscious, limiting beliefs (mental objections to being one's true self) that most people carry inside them, preventing them from embodying their free, peaceful, and connected self. These are covered below with suggestions for how to move past them.

Before going into those limiting beliefs, however, it is important to discuss the process we all go through when we're looking for transformation in any area of our lives.

THE PROCESS OF TRANSFORMATION

When you have a desire for transformation, you generally try to find answers within your current knowledge base (your memories and intellectual knowledge). If you draw a blank within your current knowledge base, maybe you seek out answers in books or a workshop. You gain some knowledge and more information, but it doesn't necessarily start to inform your 'autopilot' personality.

Finally, you realize intellectual knowledge isn't enough and you give up trying to find answers outside yourself. You decide to simply sit with it. Maybe you meditate, maybe you just let yourself fall asleep, or maybe you just completely let go of trying. In other words, you spontaneously enter an in-between moment. And when you do, *poof* you gain a direct insight into your problem; an insight that starts to infiltrate your body and mind and actually helps you make better choices for yourself.

But that insight didn't come from your current knowledge base. The insight came, well... from nowhere... didn't it? Well it's not nowhere of course, it is simply a place that is 'beyond the known.' It came from beyond the veil of consciousness and conditioned mind. It has come from your inner voice which is the embodiment of universal wisdom and creativity that exists within you. The voice that is speaking to you when you say you had an intuition.

Think back to a moment where you experienced this kind of insight. Your insights came when, in a moment of receptivity, you relaxed enough for your awareness to move beyond the mental fog and settle down in a calm and open place within you. That place of stillness is what allows you to access *the borderland*. The borderland is the place in your consciousness where what is known meets that which is 'beyond the known.' Or simply put - the *unknown*... A place where you are open to receiving new knowledge from your inner voice.

But you don't have to wait for those spontaneous moments. You can train yourself in the conscious act of entering into the borderland and receiving from beyond the known. You can learn to receive everything that you need from the inner voice in order to more fully embody your inner wisdom, freedom and experience of connection. The best part? It's going to be really easy. Because you have already had moments of great receptivity. To some degree, you have already experienced what it's like to be at peace, to be free, and to feel connected, and you have the experience of paradise and innocence deeply ingrained within you. Throughout your growth process, you have gained insights into your true nature and (consciously or unconsciously) you have already been in touch with your inner voice, even if you haven't known what it was.

Knowing that you have even some small feeling of what you want means that all you have to do is focus on that feeling, ask for more of it, receive it, and integrate it into your body. Why your body? Because your body and unconscious mind are linked - if not one and the same. Think about it, your body always reacts to what your unconscious mind is thinking. You might even say that your body *mirrors* your mind. So maybe your body *is* your mind. But whether or not you choose to view the body/mind in this way, you can't deny the connection. When your mind reacts to a situation, so does your body.

For now, however, we will think of them as separate. We will say that your mind *signals* your body to react to certain situations in the way it believes is appropriate (misguided as it may sometimes be). Your mind creates contraction and shallow breathing in your body when it is afraid and trying to prevent you from being who you truly are. When you are feeling happy, your body is open and relaxed and you breath freely.

The opposite is true as well. When you calm your body and you slow your breath, your mind also calms down and opens to a greater consciousness. And because you have conscious control over your body and breath, you can use body and breath awareness, to naturally affect your mind. You can choose, at any time, to create space in your mind by creating space in your body. It is simple: by calming your body, your mind can enter into stillness and receptivity. By breathing deeply, your mind's natural connection to its source opens.

So, from a place of calm body and open breath your consciousness can naturally and effortlessly enter into the borderland - that place in consciousness where you are just on the verge of leaving what is consciously known to you behind. From the borderland, you can enter a state of timelessness, in-between the moments, and you can receive guidance clearly from your inner voice. As you receive, you can invite your inner voice to fill up places of tension in your body, which also creates new patterns in your unconscious mind, or you can ask your inner voice to transform places in your mind, which also affects your body.

Take action: Body Awareness Meditation

Close your eyes and focus on a negative experience you have had. Observe your body's reaction to it. Now shift your focus to think about something positive you have experienced. Observe your body's reaction to it. Write down your observations.

BEYOND THE VEIL

So where is the inner voice? Where does it dwell? How do you get in touch with it other than in moments where something seems to click and it just happens? The inner voice lives *beyond the borderland*. Beyond what is consciously known to you. It is called the borderland to remind you that to reach out to the inner voice most effectively, you stand in the twilight of consciousness. You must stand on that border between the known and the unknown, invite the inner voice to come to you, and receive from it. The borderland is like the point where the Earth's atmosphere connects to space; where it can receive the rays of the sun (the inner voice), and on a clear day, filter them down to nourish life in the physical body.

The beginning of this journey to the borderland is straightforward. You use meditation to calm your body and breath. Then, standing on the edge of your known universe, you invite the inner voice over to your side of the veil. This part will feel familiar because you have already done this many times, you are just learning to do it more consciously. The next step can be more difficult because your unconscious programming begins to respond with its conditioning, limiting beliefs, fears and stories, and it feels like nothing is coming through from your inner voice.

When a message comes in from the inner voice, it is like a love note from the universe. But you know how hard it can be to receive love sometimes. The love note is like a new and alien software program approaching the inbox of your mind. Since your unconscious mind is programmed to respond to life in a specific way, it rejects the new program and resists any changes that do not compute with what it holds as truth (it tries to stay in its comfort zone). At that point, your conditioning kicks in with the 'I can't' voice and shuts down your ability to perceive the answers and changes you are inviting in.

When you allow yourself to truly receive your inner voice, you will be shaped by what is true at your core. You will receive emotional, mental and physical healing, and your personality will start changing in the ways you desire. Receiving will turn you upside down and shake out your pockets to make sure you are not carrying anything that no longer serves you. Eventually, it will remove everything that is left of your limited identity and replace it with the limitless love, creativity, and sense of connection that live inside you.

So how do you masterfully receive? The answer to that is not so much in 'how to receive,' but in what to look for when you have put your mind in a state of receptivity. Lets say you sit down, close your eyes, take a few deep breaths, become receptive, and say to yourself, 'OK, I'm ready to embody all of my insights into my true and amazing nature! Inner voice, come to me...!'

Well, maybe you perceive something happening and maybe you don't. So here's what to actually look for: You are looking for your *feeling sense*. Your feeling sense is your sixth sense. In the Buddhist tradition, there are not five senses, but six. The sixth sense is your consciousness. It is what you experience or 'feel' when you focus your attention on your non-verbal experience, and nothing else. And we'll go more into that in a moment, but first, have an experience of it.

Take action: The Feeling Sense Meditation

Close your eyes and allow your body to relax as you take deep breaths. Focus on positive experiences you have had in the past to help you become calm and open. In this place of calm, your mind automatically starts to be receptive to something beyond itself and the natural healing powers of your inner voice start to penetrate through the borderland - from beyond the known. As you allow this process to happen, let your consciousness drift into a timeless and spacious place. A place in-between the moments. This is where inspiration comes from. Allow that inspiration to pour in and experience it as a non-verbal, completely experiential feeling in your body. What was your experience?

THE FEELING SENSE

To clarify - when the word 'feeling' is used in this context, these are not emotions like anger, happiness etc... The feeling of what is in your consciousness (the 'feeling sense' as we'll call it), is similar to touch. When something touches you, you feel it or sense it. When something touches you in your consciousness, you feel it in much the same way. You feel it like you would a sensation on your skin. At least when you are awake to it.

When you are looking for a response from your inner voice, you are looking for a feeling that you can't put into words. It can come across as a subtle shift in how your body feels (temperature, flow, prickling, etc...), or as an awareness of the movement of subtle energy. A pure feeling in your consciousness has no words attached to it, nor is there a need to attach any words to it until they naturally occur. It is pure, non-verbal, experience.

Try this to help you pinpoint your feeling sense: Think about your experience of peace. You probably have ideas and even an emotional charge around it (desire for it, frustration about it disappearing when you most want it, and so forth...), but if you look beyond all those, peace is also a feeling in your consciousness. It is a non-verbal experience.

Take action:

Take a few deep breaths and feel into the *non-verbal, feeling-sense,* experience of peace.

Another perspective on understanding the feeling sense is by comparing it to how you remember something. It's as if something is on the tip of your memory, but you just can't figure it out. You have the feeling of the answer but you don't have it quite yet. 'Where did I leave my keys?' you can see them, smell them, taste them, you can *feel* where you left them, but it's just not coming to you. You sit down, close your eyes and concentrate on that feeling. When you do that, a conscious intuition starts to take shape and *poof* you remember where you left them. You were open to receiving the information.

When you stand in the borderland, between the known and the unknown, and invite help from your inner voice, you immediately receive a response. That response is a vibration that can be perceived in your consciousness as a feeling or sensation. The subtle shift in energy that you perceive (the feeling) is the beginning. It is how you start to receive an answer from your inner voice and become a master of your intuition.

Your ability to be aware of this feeling in your consciousness depends on how resistant your mind is to it. That's normal. Your perception of the response may not come as a potent, full body experience. The shift or sensation in your consciousness might seem so slight that you will tell yourself, 'no that's too weak to be it' or 'that's not how I expected it to be, so I'm dismissing it.' Your perception of a response from your inner voice may start as a very distant pinprick hole of a feeling, but as you learn to recognize it and focus your attention on it, the feeling will strengthen like a ray of light moving closer and closer. To help it grow stronger, stay aware of your feeling sense, track its movement through your body and give yourself permission to change and grow as it does; emptying a drawer of old clothes so that the new way of being can move in.

Those old clothes might be in the form of sadness, shame or resentment. They might be the way you think something is 'supposed to be.' Pay attention to your thoughts and emotions as you receive and feel, and you will see very clearly what is in the drawer that needs emptying. What the old pattern of thought is that needs to be cleared.

A not-so-subtle clue to knowing when you are in resistance is available in your body. If your breathing becomes shallow or some muscles in your body tense up, it's a sure sign there is resistance in your mind. Focus on relaxing your body and slowing your breath, and the thoughts or emotions that are causing the resistance will slowly make themselves known to you. When you see them, don't do anything. Just allow yourself to understand, and experience them until you feel a natural inclination to move on, even if they are not completely resolved. In the next chapter on creativity, we will further discuss emotional release and healing.

Journaling prompt:

What does being in the borderland mean to you?

Take action: The Borderland Meditation

Close your eyes and sink deep into yourself. Find the place within you where the known meets the unknown; find the borderland. Next, imagine you are standing in the bright sun in an open field. Then see the rays of the sun (the inner voice), traveling through the earth's atmosphere (the borderland) and into you. Ask a specific question of your inner voice and receive the answer through the rays of the sun and your feeling sense. Slowly allow the feeling of what you are receiving to travel throughout your body until it becomes words or an image in your conscious mind. Describe your experience of this practice in your journal.

WHAT YOU ARE GOING TO ENCOUNTER

When you ask for guidance or transformation - your inner voice / inner artist responds immediately with an answer. Always, it responds. The objections in your mind are what prevent you from receiving or perceiving that you are being offered something. It takes real patience and determination to see when your mind is resisting the new energy coming in from your inner voice. That is because receiving this new energy can lead to the unveiling of emotional pain, and realizations about yourself, your life and other people that your unconscious mind has been protecting you from. Body awareness is crucial at this point.

When a positive change takes place in your mind, you can feel it in your body as calm and as relaxation. When your unconscious mind blocks the bubbling up of your inner wisdom, it contracts your body and shuts down your breathing - limiting your ability to experience life. As you recall, your body and unconscious mind are linked (if not one and the same). When you re-align your body, relax your breath, and shift your awareness back to receiving, it allows the subtle vibration of the inner voice to flow in and re-wire your mind. When you let the new energy flow into your resistance directly, without interference or guidance, it will transform it without any effort on your part, as a sculptor transforms a rock.

Remember that little person inside of you holding up the wall against the tidal wave? The goal isn't to bring that wall tumbling down - that would be overwhelming. The goal is to relax your resistance long enough so you can start perceiving and receiving the gifts that are being offered to you. Walking patiently on a strategic path so that change can happen over time. You don't want to break the wall right away, you simply want to tap into the flow so that the waters within can come back to nourish you, and make your mental fields beautiful and healthy again. If you keep allowing your inner voice to flow in, it will eventually transform your mind completely in the positive ways you desire.

Journaling prompts:
1. On a scale of 1-10, how determined are you to be able to receive from your inner voice clearly and consistently?
2. Remind yourself what your motivation is (review your vision statement if need be).
3. After reminding yourself what your motivation is, try it again: On a scale of 1-10, how determined are you to be able to receive from your inner voice clearly and consistently?

ILLUMINATING YOUR RESISTANCE

Outlined in this section are a few of the most common mental objections you might find within yourself, and ways to re-gain perspective when this resistance arises. As you already know, these objections will mostly be unconscious at first. They are the reason why sometimes, when you ask a question or invite something new to flower, you don't feel anything in response, or you get overwhelmed and give up.

An 'I can't' statement is a mental objection or unconscious resistance to getting what you want, or to simply being yourself. There are millions of variations of 'I can't' statements that are all, essentially, explanations as to 'why' you can't have what you want or be yourself. No matter how stuck you feel, however, in any given situation, there is always a way through. Just remember what Albert Einstein said, "You can't solve a problem from the same state of consciousness that created it." Look beyond your limited mind to the wisdom of the inner voice to illuminate the path.

It is possible that most 'I can't' statements have become so ingrained in your identity that it's difficult to tell them apart from who you really are anymore. There are probably some deeply ingrained 'I can't' statements that are part of that person you refer to when you say 'I'. A place where you are just so used to being disconnected that you don't bother with it anymore. This remains true no matter how far you have come on your path.

Focusing on the mental objections, however, is not the primary concern. But noticing them is important, as it allows you to distinguish them from your inner voice. What is of primary importance is to start identifying the *feeling* of 'I can't' in your body. It will serve you no end by helping you reposition your mind back to the feeling of what you desire, and to have a relationship with it.

When an 'I can't' statement takes hold of your mind (no matter what the 'why' is), your body reacts as well: You lose your physical and respiratory alignment, your body becomes tense, and your breathing shallows. You might even become depressed because you can't see a path to having what you want and because you are not 'allowed' to be your authentic self.

When you get distracted by an 'I can't' statement, gently realign your body, deepen your breathing and shift your mind back into a receptive and open state. In other words, enter an *in-between moment* by inviting spaciousness and timelessness in from your inner voice. When you do, focus on the *feeling sense* and allow your inner voice to naturally melt away your tension and mental objections.

If you are interested in diving into more instances of 'why' you can't (and some specific suggestions on how to deal with them), an expanded list is included in the appendix. So that you have an idea of what these can look like in general, three examples are provided here.

I want… But I can't because…

That's not how it is supposed to feel

When you have a specific expectation of what you are looking for (of what a desired experience is supposed to look like), you block the truth from coming forward. When you have a memory of how you experienced something at one time in the past, and you think it will be the same each time, you prevent yourself from receiving the most current and most medicinal version of what you are looking for. You prevent evolution and may feel bewildered, betrayed, frustrated or hopeless.

Suggestions: Invite yourself to become comfortable with the unknown. It is only from there that you will receive new perspectives. Invite your mind to become a blank slate. Open up to your inner voice and ask, 'show me where I'm not willing to accept the gifts that are being offered to me. Help me open to the new and unknown so that I can truly open my intuition.' Then sit silently and feel the answer in your body. First, as a non-verbal experience. Then wait for the answer to become images or words in your conscious mind.

I don't want to change in this way

When you are particularly attached to a part of yourself, it is hard to let it go. Perhaps it protects you in some way. Perhaps at one point in your life it served a real purpose, or you are simply unable to perceive a 'self' without this component and that scares you. Maybe admitting this part needs to change means admitting that you held a strong belief about something for a long period of time that was wrong and it is hard to see that about yourself. You might feel afraid of change, annihilation or of seeing your own shortcomings.

Suggestions: Examine your unwillingness and the strength of your conviction. Do you really want a truthful answer to your query? Ask your inner voice: 'What habit am I attached to? What emotional pain am I numbing that I am unwilling to change? How can I strengthen my willingness to learn?' Ask to clearly and compassionately see the part of you that is still hiding. Let the answers come first in the feeling sense.

There are external circumstances that are insurmountable.

'I don't have enough cash, enough time, enough knowledge, enough supporters…' What's most important to remember in this situation is that you only have a small fraction of the information about your current circumstances. You don't know who you are going to meet around the corner. You don't know what supporters will show up if you just let the world around you know the mission you are on. If you are not willing to see how your intuition is able to guide you to the external support that you need, you might feel lonely, abandoned, resentful or depressed.

Suggestions: Imagine you are walking a pathway in a maze to get to where you want to be and you can't see around the next corner. But when you get to that corner, all you need do is ask your inner voice, 'where do I need to go *right now* to get to where I want to be?' When you ask that question with an emphasis on 'right now,' you will always receive guidance. It might be to get a cup of tea and take a break. It might be to get on a plane to Korea. Trust your inner voice like you are an investigator following clues, never really knowing where they are going to lead.

Journaling prompt:

Identify 3 primary 'I can't' statements that are alive in you right now. What does it feel like in your body when they are in control of you?

Take action:

Look up your 'I can't' statements in the appendix and apply the solutions. Describe your experience.

WHAT'S REJECTION GOT TO DO WITH IT?

"If we are going to be damned, let's be damned for what we really are!"

~ Captain Picard of the Starship Enterprise

The fear of rejection is a primal fear that every human being faces. You are, by design, a social being, and this reality is carefully wired into your DNA. There is no greater fear than being rejected by the tribe because without it you have no food, shelter, connection, and love. In fact, it is possible that at the root of every fear or unconscious resistance to change is the primal fear of rejection.

It is important to remember that the experience of rejection is real whether the rejection itself is real, imagined or an innocent child's interpretation of something harmless. As a child, your brain absorbed an enormous amount of information. Literally - it absorbed it (or received it). The undeveloped brain of a child has no filters and no capacity for interpreting information as anything other than truth. If, as a child, you perceived that you needed to be anything other than your true self to feel safe and loved (and let's face it - we all did), you likely made an unconscious choice to create an artificial self. You constructed yourself based on the influences of those who you were dependent on, and whose care you desired.

It is natural that as you grow older you continue to carry an unconscious fear of being rejected by the people who shaped you, even though many changes you make in yourself won't necessarily mean that you will be rejected. Sometimes, however, it happens - you decide to make a change and actually have to face rejection when you decide to be true to yourself! Be it from the people you are most intimate with or from those who you consider your friend and acquaintances.

In order to truly thrive, you may have to accept that experiencing the temporary loneliness of rejection is better than experiencing a lifetime of oppression. Trust that when it is time to evolve, you will evolve into new and better relationships and more supportive networks that reflect your new reality. Effectively, that you will find a new tribe that better fits with who you naturally are instead of one where you are constantly trying to appease and fit it.

If you are feeling resistance within you that won't melt away, you can inquire: 'Who am I afraid will reject me if I restore this lost piece of myself? Who has already rejected me for it?' You will see that inside of you there is a statement that looks something like this: 'I am afraid of *so-and-so* rejecting me, so I have to be *this other way that is not me* to please them.'

Once you see who this is, you will most likely have an emotional reaction and feel the sadness of that internal rejection and disconnection. When you do, focus on building your pillar of connection by turning to that source of love and nourishment within you for healing so that you don't get caught in the trap of feeling isolated. On the more hopeful side: Making changes in ourselves inevitably gives permission to others to do so as well, even if at first they don't understand. In the long run, they will be grateful for your courage and for reflecting that being your true and authentic self is absolutely possible.

It is exciting to offer the light within you to the world in exactly the way you naturally shine. You can do it! You can have all the resistance to your true nature completely and miraculously erased. And by doing so, you give permission to others to do it as well.

Take action:
Say this out loud: 'I can have all my resistance to my true nature, completely and miraculously erased!'

No really... Say it!
What is the non-verbal feeling of that in your body (the *feeling sense*)? Also notice what happens if the unconscious 'I can't' statements try to take over. You will know this is going on if your body starts to contract or shrink. If a sinking feeling or even dread comes over you.

Becoming yourself again is a process. It starts by identifying that initial feeling you get in your body when you set a positive intention in your mind and then becoming aware of your resistance to it.

Journaling prompts:
1. When you say the words above, and then feel contraction in your body, indicating resistance in your mind, ask yourself, 'Who am I afraid will reject me if I restore this lost piece of myself, and why? Who has already rejected me for it?' Complete this sentence (as many times as is applicable): 'I am afraid of *so-and-so* rejecting me, so I have to be *this other way that is not me* to please them.'
2. Where in your life are you limiting yourself because of a fear of rejection?

SO WHERE DO I START?

All this begs the question: 'What is the best intention to set for myself?' An important takeaway for you to have is this: There are two places from which your desires and intentions arise: The conditioned mind, and your intuition, which is the expression of your inner voice.

If you choose, you can set your intention using one of these statements (or any variation that suits you): 'What evolution does my inner voice want for me? What does *it* want me to see? Who does my inner voice want me to become? Inner voice, what is the one thing I can receive now, that will make all my resistance to my true self melt away?' You can invite the inner voice to sculpt you into a particular form - into something that *you* think is good. Or you can invite your inner voice to see the best in you, uncover it, and surprise you with the splendor of it.

That being said, everybody faces specific challenges in life. These are places where you feel stuck and where you are desperate to find solutions. These places can serve as doorways for you - opportunities for personal growth and for gaining awareness. Some examples include: 'I just had a fight with my partner (that same old fight we always have).' If this happens, next time you have a chat with your inner voice, ask for a new insight and understanding about this issue.

Another example: 'I just can't get clients for my new business.' Next time you practice, ask about this and receive a new vibration (new information) about it. No problem is too small. In fact, if you are telling yourself that something within you shouldn't get attention, it is a dead giveaway that that is where you should focus your attention.

When you work with an intention, commit to working with it consistently over a period of time rather than flopping around. Repetition and discipline are what will create real change, because repetition is what will make changes to your brain and therefore, to your actions. Brain research has clearly shown that you can learn something once, and it will create new networks of neural-pathways. However, it has also shown that without repetition and consistent practice those new pathways will disintegrate, and the old ingrained patterns will stay in control.

To anchor new behaviors - repetition and body-memory are crucial. So you have to work regularly with your intentions and the practices. To create a new path for yourself, you literally need to change your brain. For this - repetition is crucial; and involving your body is crucial. Did we say that already?

Take action: Answering Your Questions Meditation

Think of a situation in your life where you need new insight. Close your eyes, head into the borderland (even if you haven't had a clear experience of it yet) and ask your inner voice for insight. Become aware of your feeling sense as you do - your subtle body awareness. Allow the sensations to unfold, being open and willing to change and grow to receive answers. What was your experience?

Journaling prompt:

In the practices you have done so far connecting to your inner voice at the borderland, what are the main insights you have gained into the process of receiving intuitions from your inner voice?

CHANGE

Yes, change is scary. But living life as a trained monkey is even more scary. Being afraid of the unknown won't get you what you want. Not even close. It is in daring to explore the unknown, and daring to become something completely new that you finally get closer to understanding the great mystery of life and what it means to be alive.

In order to build a temple for your inner voice in your body, become as receptive as a child. Absorb the vibration being offered to you by your inner voice in the same way a child's brain absorbs it's environment. As an adult, you get to decide who programs you and creates you anew. You get to choose to let your inner voice uncover the greatness within you.

Remember Albert Einstein's quote, "You can't solve a problem from the same state of consciousness that created it." Turn the wheel over to a greater awareness within you and *receive*. You contain an infinite well of wisdom and beauty, and the one thing that will completely transform your life is to have permanent and direct access to it! Practice receiving from your inner voice regularly, and it will become second nature to fully embody and be that voice. Let the gifts from within you fill you up and overflow into the world.

Take action:

Make a commitment to regularly practice becoming receptive to your inner voice. What is your practice going to consist of? When and how often are you going to do it? Do you need an accountability buddy to keep you on track? Do you need to set alarms on your phone? What is your commitment?

TAKING BACK THE IN-BETWEEN

The problem with a lack of receptivity isn't time, remember? It is a need to be in control. To help you realize this and build your pillar of receptivity, establish the habit of taking back the *physical* in-between moments of your life. What are physical in-between moments?

A physical in-between moment is:

- when you are sitting in your car, about to drive off.
- when you arrive somewhere.
- when you are going to the bathroom.
- when you are waiting at the checkout line.
- when you have lost your car keys.
- when there is a train going by.
- when you are waiting for somebody.
- when you are waiting for your food at a restaurant.
- when you are about to relax and then you remember something you need to do.

There are a lot of physical in-between moments in your day. You will soon find them all and start using the physical in-between moments to enter into the *spiritual* in-between moments. That mystical place of stillness, spaciousness, and receptivity from where inspiration, vitality, and creativity arise.

The following is a 30-second practice to do in those physical in-between moments (or some personalized variation of this):

Living In-Between the Moments Meditation

1. Take 2 deep breaths while thinking: "I am doing a lot of things right in my life, I am not perfect, and I don't need to be completely in control. I can receive support from my inner voice." Or simply say, 'I can receive support from my inner voice!"
2. Pause after your 2 breaths and stay silent for a moment.
3. Say to yourself: "I am capable of living in a way that nourishes me."
4. Become receptive to the feelings you want to have in your life and receptive to the feeling of paradise.
5. Say to yourself: "Everything that life offers me can make me wiser and happier."
6. Become aware of your *feeling sense* and feel the energy changing in your body. Even if you can't put a finger on what exactly is different. Feel that something is changing and then move on with your day.

LIVING IN-BETWEEN THE MOMENTS – AN EXPLANATION OF THE PRACTICE

When you have an in-between moment, instead of being worried about time or looking at your phone, you are going to take about 30 seconds to take 2 deep breaths and build the pillar of receptivity in your life. You will create a new experience for yourself based on the feelings you want to experience. One suggestion for your intention in this practice is: experiencing the feelings of spaciousness, safety, home, gratitude, and co-creative flow. Or simply put, experiencing paradise within.

The solution isn't in turning around one thought or feeling here and there, it's in creating a new pattern for yourself during these in-between moments. As you practice, these feelings will start to grow and slowly infiltrate all areas of your life. When you create that new pattern by receiving from your inner voice, all the negative thinking will organically fall away. To that end, during your physical in-between moments, you will really start to embrace receptivity. You will say to yourself, "I am doing a lot of things right in my life, I am not perfect, and I don't need to be completely in control. I can receive support from my inner voice."

If you are not perfect and not in control then you can let go a little bit or, at least, you will start to feel that it's possible. You will start getting re-connected to the mystical experience of a spiritual in-between moment - that all-encompassing sense of spaciousness and timelessness. Affirming this to yourself means you can really start opening to a feeling of trust in the unexpected gifts that your inner voice has to offer.

Next, you will remind yourself that: "I am capable of living in a way that nourishes me." When making this statement, you are planting seeds that will allow you to do all the same activities you are doing now, but from a place of ease, gratitude, and faith instead of urgency and scarcity.

By affirming this intention for yourself, you will start to develop a partnership with the unknown forces outside of your conscious control. After all, just because the universe is chaotic, it doesn't mean you can't work with it. Dancing with the unknown is powerful, so to affirm you are capable of being an amazing dance partner you will add: "Everything life offers can make me wiser and happier."

Note: In doing this practice, feel free to change the words to any that resonate for you. Or instead of using any words at all in this practice, simply open to a non-verbal state of receptivity, timelessness, and spaciousness and see what your inner voice has to offer you.

THE KEY TO EVERYTHING

When you do this 30-second practice there is a secret you will need to learn for it to be effective. Implementing this specific change in your mind is going to be the difference between a life of chasing something you can't ever seem to catch, and a life where you not only accomplish everything on your list, you also witness miracles along the way. As stated, the words aren't important - change them to anything that you resonate with or get rid of them entirely.

True transformation takes place only when you are in a place of receptivity and in relationship with your inner voice. So, when you say your affirmations, do so from a place of willingness to change, a place of receptivity, and with an open invitation to be in relationship with the feelings you want to have in your life. This is the only way to create a new pattern. Remember, you can't make changes in yourself from your conscious mind because it is like asking a rock to sculpt *itself*. But there is a place of creativity – a higher consciousness within you that you can call on to re-create your mind and give you the experiences you want to have. The process is one of co-creation! The desire, receptivity, and willingness to change come from your conscious mind, and the transformation is created by your inner voice as a response to your desire.

Take action:

Do the in-between the moments practice right now. What insight did you gain from the practice?

THE BRAIN DUMPING SOLUTION

Between now and when you finally anchor that feeling of spaciousness in your life there is an easy to implement, practical solution you might try called Brain Dumping. One of the biggest stressors you might have is not that you have a long to-do list. The biggest stressor is that you are going to forget about something important on that list or that you are not going to prioritize things correctly.

So… are you feeling stressed out? Trying to rest but can't? Dump your brain onto paper by making a list of everything you need to do. If you like, you can make several lists having to do with various projects you are working on and then make a master list of the smaller lists. You can also take things off the project lists and move them onto a 'First Priority' list. Even if you never end up looking at the list again (which is okay), the stress relieving function of this simple act will make a huge difference.

The other form of brain dumping is less practical and more emotional and mental. Make a list of all the emotions circulating within you. Make another list of all your thoughts. The emotions and thoughts don't have to make sense. They don't even have to be completely true and accurate. If you are thinking it or feeling it, put it down on paper. If you are furious, if you are happy, if you are embarrassed about that hat you wore… write down anything and everything. Then, of course, burn it, shred it or otherwise make sure that it doesn't fall into the hands of your friends, co-workers, kids, partner or The New-York Times.

Take action:

Can you make a commitment to yourself to do this next time you are feeling stressed out and overwhelmed?

YOUR LEGACY & A HEALTHY STATE OF MIND

There are a lot of unknowns in your world when it comes to letting go. You are rightfully worried, but know that everything you want to do can be taken care of from a healthy state of mind. You can still be the busiest person on the planet if you choose to be. You just don't want that busyness to come from the fear of losing control and the fear of being imperfect.

You will never be in complete control of your world and you will never be perfect. Ever! Also, you will never accomplish everything you set out to. Everybody dies with a to-do list. Your life's work continues beyond your individual human lifetime. Unfinished business is simply a part of life. It will never all be done, so there is no point chasing it until your last breath.

That said, thinking big is what leaving behind your legacy is all about, so never stop doing that! An ability to think big is one of the gifts of building your pillar of receptivity. But unless you learn to do it all with a sense of spaciousness (aware of how every moment is an in-between moment), your life might be too short for the legacy you want to leave to take root.

We all do what we can with the time we have. What is most important is *how* we do it. The energy with which you plant seeds becomes the nutrients the plant is fortified with. In those in-between moments, remember that no one ever died thinking of all the days they spent making sure nothing fell apart (if anything, they regret them). What you reflect on at the end of your life (and at the end of your day) are the moments of inspiration you had. You remember the moments of love you shared when you took extra time to invest in what really matters. When you chose process over schedule. At the end of your day, you will find it remarkable how, when you stepped back into an in-between moment, miraculously, The Blissful Intelligence of the Universe showed up with solutions that you never would have thought of on your own.

Letting life support you not only makes *your* life better, it plants the seeds that makes the world around you better as well. Because the inner voice that acts through you, is the same inner voice that acts through everybody. The same inner voice that allows *you* to be creative, allows *everybody* to be creative. Ultimately, we are all working on the same project: The future of Earth. And this creative project is the most important part of life, as it leads you to the experience of living a life of purpose.

Journaling Prompt:

Who are the people you know or have met that you believe have a strong pillar of receptivity? What can you learn from them?

Take action:

Ask the people you know who have a strong pillar of receptivity for advice on building yours. Reach out to at least one person right now. Journal about the advice they give.

BUILDING THE PILLAR OF CREATIVITY

THE PILLAR

While building the pillar of creativity, you may find yourself overburdened with circling thoughts ('head-chatter') and a feeling of emptiness. The bad kind of emptiness, not the fertile kind. The kind of emptiness where you can't ever seem to attain that which you desire. The kind of emptiness that comes from repeatedly trying to feel happy but always falling short.

This kind of emptiness where you are lost in a maze of thoughts, has a very specific cause. The cause is a wounded heart and an inability to fully experience your own emotions - a kind of numbness. So, the first step to building your pillar of creativity is to open your heart and dive in. And the second step, is to emerge out of the other side of your heart into the great *fertile* emptiness and silence within you. The kind of silence that you attain when you fully experience your emotions and are able to receive from your connection to a source of nourishment within. When you give yourself access to this fertile emptiness within you, you become a true *weaver* of creation. When you weave from the infinite pool of potential in your heart, your creativity naturally flows and births new ideas in your current area of passion.

When you open your heart, you gain access to your genius. In the spiritual realms think of poets like Indian mystic Mira Bai and the Sufis Rumi and Hafiz as being truly connected to their creativity with an unburdened and silent heart. Spiritually awake artists like Alex Grey come to mind as well. But you can find examples of truly inspired creators in any field. They are the joyful kindergarten teacher down the street and the scattered scientist you had as a professor in college. They are even the high tech geek who never leaves his computer because he is developing the next generation of computing.

When you have built your pillar of creativity, you are able to see the infinite patterns of life strung throughout the universe. You can follow them in your imagination and weave together new and inspirational things. This is how genius is born, and it all starts with unburdening your heart and opening it to the true *spiritual* experience of emptiness that is the primordial soup of creation, containing an infinity of potential and possibility within it.

Take action: The Well Meditation

Close your eyes and focus your attention at the center of your chest. Imagine a little 'you' is standing there, at your heart center. Now imagine an infinitely deep well next to that little you. Next, take a few deep breaths, dive into the well and swim all the way down, until you emerge from the other side. Describe your experience in your journal.

Note: Silence and fertile emptiness can seem like 'nothing' at first. So, if you experience nothing, ask yourself if you are ignoring the experience of silence and fertile emptiness because you are expecting it to be different. Remember to pay attention to your feeling sense and ask your inner voice to assist you in this process.

Journaling prompts:

1. What are your thoughts about this statement: Anywhere you find genius, you find receptivity to the vast pool of potential within.
2. What is *your* genius when you are tuned into the vast pool of potential within? List anything and everything no matter how big or how small or whether you think it will make you world famous or simply a happier person.

THE CHALLENGE: NUMB, FROZEN, AND IMMOBILE

When you are still in the process of building your pillar of creativity, the voices inside your head might feel like ghosts, calling to you at all hours of the day and night. Those voices remind you of things that have happened and imagine possible things to come with equal determination. The thoughts can be persistent and constant. They can make you feel like you are at the edge of your seat – jumpy, and easily startled. Most importantly perhaps, they affect your ability to sleep, rest, and enjoy life.

Some of these thought cycles include:

- Reviewing an action you took or something you witnessed
- Going in circles, trying to decide about something
- Doubting yourself
- Fears about what will happen if…
- Wondering what other people think
- Negative self-talk
- Predictions of failure
- Wondering how to achieve a goal and feeling frustrated
- Seeing images of past traumatic experiences (real, televised or imagined)

The head chatter is a kind of defense mechanism your unconscious mind uses to avoid fully experiencing the world around you. After all, the fear that creates this kind of head chatter is the fear of exposure. The kind of exposure you feel when your heart is wide open and tender. Vulnerable to pain and grateful for joy. A heart that is present and never runs away no matter what it must face. The kind of exposure you felt when you had that dream about being naked on stage in front of a huge audience.

When your pillar of creativity is still being built, you may feel frozen and numb, and unable to weave and create. It is because these circling thoughts and the fear of exposure render you exactly that – numb, frozen, and immobile. In extreme situations, this 'head chatter' not only affects your ability to hear and follow your inner voice, it also affects your ability to trust people and receive their affection. It prevents you from building your pillars of connection and receptivity. You might be so lost in those circling thoughts that you can't see how much love and tenderness is being showered on you. You might be so afraid of being seen (afraid of exposure) that you hide and protect your heart from everything and anything no matter how good or how bad it is.

Journaling prompt:
What kinds of head chatter do you tend to experience (from the list above or anything else)?

Take action:
Next time you experience head chatter in your daily life, do the Well Practice above. Will you make a commitment to yourself to do that?

Take action: Fear of Exposure Meditation
Close your eyes and tune into your fear of exposure. The fear of being seen for exactly who you are. Seen in your shame and seen in your beauty. Seen in you comfort and seen in your discomfort. Just feel that fear for a while. When you are ready, write down the thoughts that circle in your mind when you feel the fear.

COMPETITION

Having a fear of exposure could indicate that you suffer from a mild state of trauma. This can be something deep and formative such as abuse in your childhood years. It could be from bullying in school or another violent incident. But it doesn't have to be something specific that happened to you. The simple fact that everyone in the world is in constant competition for power, position and resources can be traumatic in and of itself. This can cause if not trauma, then simply living in a state of constant unconscious fear.

In addition to real-life violent and competitive situations, you are constantly being inundated with *stories* of violence both through fictional television shows and books, and non-fiction via the news. Your unconscious mind doesn't know the difference between something it sees on television and what happens in reality. The emotional consequences are the same. The pain accumulates in your heart and becomes too much of a burden to carry, so the heart goes numb.

Another widely unrecognized source of trauma nearly all people have today is a lack of connection with nature. Over-use of caffeine, drugs and alcohol and eating low quality (or outright destructive) foods can also put your body into a state of anxiety and tension. This leads to fatigue and a heart that cannot process its emotions properly. It leads to an experience of feeling numb and stuck.

Our natural orientation is to form community and trust rather than to isolate and compete, and deviating from what is natural is traumatic. From bullying in the schoolyard to competition at work, even small acts of rejection or violence can make the world feel hostile. These experiences shut down your heart and put your adrenals (and mental activity) into overdrive. The constant unconscious fear or anxiety hijacks the attention center of the brain (physiologically *and* experientially) and makes you constantly think about those things you are worried about and where you are afraid of being exposed to more pain.

Have compassion for yourself. We live in a world where this kind of pain is not acknowledged. We live in a world where people are so afraid of each other that disconnection is an epidemic; a world where we are taught that we have to do it all ourselves which goes against every natural social instinct we have. Be kind to yourself. Receive love and nourishment from the source within you and slowly start to open your heart to its fullest potential.

Journaling prompts:
1. What, in your present-day life, makes you feel scared (list 5-10)? These could be things you do, are exposed to, people you know, anything…
2. What memories of your past cause you to feel afraid in the present (when you think about them), even though they are only memories (list 5-10)?

WHAT EVERYBODY ELSE IS THINKING

When there is an unconscious state of trauma, there is a natural tendency to hide and protect yourself. There also exists an over-sensitivity to everyday conflict. When still building your pillar of creativity, to better cope with the world, it's possible you have learned to see into other people's minds and figure out what everybody else is thinking (or at least feeling). You may have developed this empathic (or psychic) ability to be able to appease people and fit in, thereby avoiding being your authentic, creative, self. If you can be in everybody's head, you can maneuver yourself in between other people's trajectories and avoid getting run over.

The internalized voices of other people's desires and expectations, however, are often in conflict with the voice that rises from the deep well within you. When your true self is kicking and screaming to be heard but your fear of exposure won't allow it, your thoughts are trapped and have nowhere to go for expression and resolution. This is the cause of the head-chatter that starts up when your pillar of creativity isn't built yet. You get head chatter when your thoughts are caged between your authentic inner voice and the person you are trying to force yourself to be to fit in, or be accepted. Over time, those thoughts start to back up and eventually create a swamp that can lead to feeling numb.

In this situation, your consciousness is being pulled between two powerful magnets. One is presence based and one is fear based – one positive and one negative. The voice within is constantly trying to rise and shed its light on the world to remind you of how you really want to walk, be and create. The voice of fear is constantly looking outside of you and trying to figure out how to keep from getting hurt.

When you let go of one of those two voices, the thoughts eventually subside. You might surrender your creativity completely and become repressed and numb or you can decide to allow your emotions, inner silence and creativity to be your guide. You can decide to heal yourself, and return to your natural single-minded consciousness! It is not a painless process, but facing that process is better than continuing to face the daily torment of being out of harmony with your own heart and ability to weave your genius in the world.

Take action:

Close your eyes and imagine what it would be like to let go of the fear that might be keeping you repressed. Feel the flow of creativity rise from within your heart and move through your body when you let go of fear. Feel how it naturally does so, without any effort on your part. Describe your experience in your journal.

UNSHAKABLE

Your ability to be an inspired weaver and to create from a place of harmony may be blocked by a wall of circling thought and a fear of exposure. So what can you do to become a weaver and creator again? The solutions below are relatively simple. However, it's possible you might feel uncomfortable when you start to implement them.

Some of the suggestions may even appear to exacerbate the problem at first. The apparent exacerbation of the problem happens because all that head chatter in your mind needs to be processed and cleared out. All the toxic thoughts and images need to be witnessed and the emotional experiences honored.

Remember, the spinning thoughts are not the problem, the fear of exposure is. This is good, because it means that there is no need to address the thoughts directly. The head chatter is merely a bunch of thoughts with nowhere to go. Once you give them somewhere to go, then they will... they'll go!

The key to everything is an unshakable belief in *the rightness of being who you are.* Do you have an unshakable belief in the rightness of being who you are? No matter how weak that belief might be for you, it's a certainty that on some level, you have. So ask yourself, 'Right now, this very moment, on a scale of 1-10, how strong is my belief in the rightness of being who I am?' Is it a 1? A 5? A fully built creativity pillar of 10?

What is your answer?

It is at the very core of every person's being to want to be true to who they are and do what they have come here to do. Every person deserves to explore the world and weave it in their own way, supported by the inherent goodness of their inner voice. It's only a matter of uncovering that goodness.

It is a human right to be one's self without harassment, oppression or fear of any kind. So no matter what number you came up with for your belief in the rightness of being who you are, hold on to the level of belief you have and cultivate it. There are several steps further down that will help you.

WITHDRAWAL

The head chatter you experience can also be viewed as a *withdrawal symptom!* That is why it shows up when you are trying to rest, in moments of stress, or when you are trying to gain insight into a problem you are having. To understand this better, turn to your body for an example. Your body rids itself of toxins through a process of cleansing. There are toxins buried deep in the fat cells and tissues of your body. These toxins are released when you change your exercise, eating and drinking habits.

At first, the detox is uncomfortable. You might experience skin rashes, digestive issues, and headaches as the poisons are released into your bloodstream on their way out of your body. And if your level of toxicity is bad, the symptoms can be worse. To suppress the detox all you have to do is go back to eating junk food and having a sedentary lifestyle. Essentially, to stop taking action in the right direction.

The same principle applies to your mind. When you rest your mind from external stimuli, all the thoughts and emotions you need to process start coming to the surface. The natural healing power of your inner voice comes roaring up like a wave rising inside of you to push out the toxic beliefs and painful memories. Simply put, you can think of it as taking out the trash. Or Spring cleaning.

Your heart can spit out every oppressive thought and feeling that has piled up and clogged the creativity well. You just need to surrender to the detoxification process. And like detoxing from a drug, or from a lifelong habit of fast food restores your health, detoxing your mind restores your mental clarity, and crystal clear inner voice. It's not a comfortable process, but it's a necessary one. It restores you to a direct connection with your inner voice and ability to weave creatively in the world.

When you start your detox, shame and regret are sure to pop up because you will want to blame yourself and others for your situation. But shame and regret are just more noise in your mind. More head-chatter. Leave them be, and don't let yourself get caught up in avoidance and 'I can't' voices. Instead, hold to your vision for yourself, turn to the spaciousness that lives in-between the moments, connect, and receive nourishment and love from the source within you. Then allow your emotions to flow: as tears, as sadness, as dance, as rage, as laughter, as prayer, as art… Whatever is natural for you.

Journaling prompt:
Can you relate to the description of 'head-chatter' as a detoxification process? How do you interpret that or understand it in your personal context?

Take action: Healing The Heart Meditation
Close your eyes and take a few breaths. Bring your vision for yourself and the world to mind. Then turn to the spaciousness in-between the moments, connect, and receive nourishment and love from the source within you. There, invite your inner voice to help you with the unburdening of your heart and allowing your emotions to flow. Next, visualize yourself standing in an open and sunny field. The rays of the sun (representing the inner voice) traveling through the borderland of the atmosphere and coming into your body. Take your time receiving the sun's rays and observe your feeling sense as you receive the sunlight.

Describe your experience in your journal.

PURSUING DISTRACTIONS

To recap: If you are having an issue with head chatter blocking your inner voice, it may be the result of the healing power of your mind trying to process an overload of thoughts and feelings. But you can easily stop the process of this mental detox and squash your innate healing powers. To stop the process all you have to do is watch television, throw yourself into figuring out a problem, clean something, get into conflict with somebody who doesn't deserve it, complain about something, behave in a way that you know to be toxic, etc…

Allowing your fear of exposure to turn on the external drama and focus on things it has no control over will temporarily suppress the welling up from within, creating the appearance of relief. But you will have to pay for it eventually. There is a tug of war between your natural desire to heal and open, and the fear that wants to maintain a wall around you. All you need do for the natural, regenerative powers of your body to kick in is to stop yourself from pursuing distractions.

A simple way to support this process is to allow your external world to mirror what you would like your internal world to be by making it calm, peaceful, and natural. The benefits of a calm and natural environment on mental clarity and feelings of peace and creativity is a given. It's not news, it's just not all that easy sometimes.

Things you can do to allow the natural process of detoxification of your mind to unfold include:

1. Bashing your television in with a baseball bat: Even shows that are not based on violence are based on the creation of conflict and drama, which are not aligned with your natural state. It's not just that you won't have anything toxic to watch anymore, but the actual act of destruction will be highly cathartic and rewarding!
2. Cancel your Netflix account.
3. Delete all the news apps on your phone.
4. Spend time sitting or lying down on the earth every day (even just two minutes).
5. Take a hike where there is no electricity or go camping off-grid (nature is the best therapist).
6. Figure out whose thoughts you have been thinking, because they certainly aren't yours (more on this below).
7. Start to draw a picture in your mind (or on paper) of the person who is underneath all those thoughts (more on this below).
8. Contemplate the rightness of being who you are!
9. Be kind to yourself. Remind yourself that this is a difficult and very courageous process. You deserve love, tenderness, and respect for even thinking about it.

Of course, you don't have to be extreme. You can take a 2-day media fast and go on a 2-hour hike and see if something within you relaxes. If some remembrance of your own creative and tender heart occurs, you know you are on the right track. And as you proceed through your 2-day cleanse, remember, the head chatter is not the problem, your *fear of exposure* is the problem. When the head chatter starts, remind yourself that it is merely your mind processing everything it needs to in order for your powerful inner voice to come forward and lead your life. Give it the chance, and it certainly will.

Also remember that you are your own greatest critic. When you fear exposure it is your own imagination of what others will say that creates the negativity. So with no toxic distractions available to you, your circling thoughts will start to come out of the ground like zombies to attack you. If you feel like being playful, you can imagine yourself pushing the zombies back into the ground as they come at you. And even if your thoughts are arguing with each other – just let them. Think of it as zombies attacking zombies. Observe all your reactions to your reactions to your reactions (the zombie rumble) and contemplate the rightness of being who you are. That's all there is to do!

On the one hand, it's good news that all you need do is stop ingesting poison and allow your natural healing system to take its course. On the other hand, well, let's just say it can be a really big challenge. Fear and panic have a way of hijacking the attention center in the brain and making you do things you know (on some level) aren't in your best interest. It's not just a psychological experience, it's a neurological one. Your brain is wired to give fear-based thoughts priority in determining where attention goes. It's a mechanism that helps ensure your survival. It's not easy to overcome, but it's not impossible either.

When the head chatter starts, one option is to just observe and do the Healing the Heart practice above. Another option is to take a deeper look at the thoughts themselves, recognizing that you most likely started to worry about something. Once you pinpoint exactly what you are worrying about, you can calm yourself down. You can either figure out what to do about it (in which case you don't have to worry anymore), or you can come to the realization that it's out of your control (in which case you don't have to worry about it anymore).

It's possible you have spent many years living in fear and busyness and that you don't have a clue what your mind looks like underneath the surface. Sometimes, it's not pretty. Sometimes, clearing out your mind means you must face painful experiences or bad choices you have made. Sometimes you must face negative beliefs about yourself. It's not easy, and it takes time. But you either do it or keep living out of fear, stuck in the numb shell of being a victim. Contemplating the rightness of being who you are will keep you going. And doing the Brain Dumping exercise from the pillar of receptivity will also provide some relief.

Journaling prompts:
1. When you contemplate the rightness of being who you are, what does it feel like?
2. Right now, what will it take to get your level of belief in the rightness of being who you are up to the next level? Up by one notch? Maybe even up by half a notch. Or by 0.0001? What will it take?

Take action: The Zombie Thoughts Meditation
Do the zombie visualization. Close your eyes and observe your thoughts. When a thought comes up, see it as a zombie and shove it back into the ground. If you don't like visualizing zombies, simply see yourself standing in front of the thought, holding your hand up and saying, 'no!' Describe your experience.

Journaling prompt:
List at least 5-10 things you can do to express kindness, appreciation, love, and support for yourself on this journey.

Take action:

Circle at least 2 things on the list above, and offer them to yourself within the next 48 hours.

OVERCOMING YOUR DESIRE FOR PARTICULAR OUTCOMES

Implementing the above suggestions for removing over-stimulation and putting yourself in nature-rich environments is the beginning (to whatever degree you are comfortable taking that leap). Doing that will give you the space you need to be more aware of yourself without continuing the suppression. Always remember that the first step in overcoming the fear of exposure is having absolute faith in the rightness of being your authentic self. Without that faith, you may not persevere through the discomfort. The second thing you will need to overcome is your desire for particular outcomes. And you will find that the two things are related.

Here's an example: Your inner voice might tell you that it's safe to speak your mind about certain injustices you see in your workplace. Your conscious mind perceives the intuition and might assume you are safe to follow your inner voice. It assumes the outcome is going to be that the injustices are addressed. Despite your fear to the contrary, you move forward and speak up. But the outcome turns out to be that you get fired and find yourself looking for a new job.

When you follow your inner voice, the results are unknown. Faith that comes from the stillness in your heart is your greatest ally in these situations. Cultivate unwavering faith that your inner voice will always aim to upgrade your life, even if it has to tear down that which is oppressing you first (no matter how familiar, comfortable and 'safe' it is). No matter what kind of journey you end up on, following that voice will be a greater and more exciting adventure than you can ever imagine.

You are capable of developing absolute faith in your inner voice to such a degree that you will follow it off a cliff. It's not the possible outcome that should be motivating you, but rather knowing the absolute rightness of doing what is true in your heart, regardless of outcome, that should be your motivation. You *can* have faith in your truth, and you can walk through life determined to do and be what is right and what is truthful. Some people who have done this have inspired millions. Other people who have done this remain completely anonymous, living simple lives yet being inspirations to those around them. Outcome doesn't matter. Being *you,* does! Because the ripple effect of being *you* is what matters.

Journaling prompt:

Was there a time in your life when you followed what was right regardless of consequence? How did that feel to you? If you can't remember a specific time, imagine what it might feel like to have that kind of integrity. Describe the events and the outcome.

A BURNING DESIRE TO SEE YOUR DENTIST

Another reason it's hard to shed your fears, overcome your head chatter, and follow your inner voice is that the results you get are not an immediate reflection of the effort you make. When learning how to overcome your fear of exposure, it's not like touching a stove and then feeling the burn. Instead, you act to unplug from external distractions, but the result is an unpleasant detox. As if instead of touching the stove and burning yourself, you felt good for a while before the burn pain kicked in. Another analogy might be getting acupuncture, where you experience a little pain in order to feel well in the long run.

Going to the dentist is another example. You don't go to the dentist and then feel good while you are there. You go, feel discomfort, and then after a while, feel clean and good. The neurons in your brain that would associate the positive result with the action aren't active together, so they are not creating networks together. This is why you never develop a burning desire to see your dentist. You never develop a direct association between *dentist* and *feeling good*. Intellectually, you know the truth, but you are not hard wired for it. And you never will be unless you create this link in a focused way by thinking about it regularly.

Your body-mind learns in a very simple way – by cause and immediate effect. When the cause and effect are distanced from each other, you need to meditate on the cause and effect aspect so that your body and mind get it. Right now, if you removed yourself from all unnecessary stimulation and went camping for 2 days, your mind might spin around in circles for a while and then finally find some rest after unwinding from habitual patterns.

This experience, however, creates a mental (hard-wired) connection between your actions and the potential unpleasantness of the cleansing. Your automated system of memory only makes that first connection. It can take many repetitions of the action or of thinking about the process repeatedly to create the neural link between going camping and feeling good. Or between moving your body and feeling good. And meanwhile, while you are creating that link, you have to operate on pure faith. Faith in the rightness of being who you are!

Your task is to create a mental bridge between the actions you take and the resulting pleasantness that comes after the detoxification of your mind. You do this by imagining the action and the feeling of the eventual outcome together. As you do this kind of mental pairing, you will become more and more hard-wired to desire the actions that create a calm mind. By generating this direct experience of causation in your mind you are going to find more and more motivation to free yourself and connect to the creative voice of your heart.

To do this practice and create these new neural networks, be a scientist. Your research questions are: What happens when I unplug? What happens when I lay on the earth? What happens when I start making a list of 'whose thoughts are these anyway?' What happens when I don't resist the rising tide of my true self welling up within me, pushing out all the junk it's buried under? Do I eventually start to feel more free? Does the real me start to come out?' You will be asking the questions and mentally drawing a direct line that bridges the discomfort and pairs up the action with the eventual result.

Take action: A Bridge to Silence Meditation

Think of the action of silencing your phone and connecting with nature as the cause of the calm that comes after the mind chatter stops. Just think about it for a while - until you feel something settle in your body. If the head chatter starts up while you are thinking about it, take strength from contemplating the rightness of being who you are. You can also ask yourself what you are worried about. Or you can take yourself into an in-between moment and into receptivity and connection. Go back to the original thought experiment when the chatting subsides. Describe your experience.

Journaling prompt:

During the practice you just did, did you feel the healing power of your mind come welling up from within you? If not, do that practice again, this time with a focus on being aware of the healing power that wants to naturally rise from within you when you unplug. Describe the experience of having the healing power rise from within you when your mind is calm.

WHOSE THOUGHTS ARE THESE ANYWAY?

You have learned how creating a bridge between your actions and the positive results can help you. Below are a couple more exercises you can do to help get over the mental chatter and fear of exposure:

Whose Thoughts Are These Anyway?

Most of the ways you think about things are inherited or copied from other people. In this exercise, you are looking for the person who influenced a specific way of thinking in you. Having this kind of perspective will help free you from their grasp. Do this practice especially when you are experiencing circling thoughts or head chatter.

Start by making a list of the thoughts in your head (positive or negative – it doesn't matter). Write down at least 5-10 thoughts. Next to each thought write the name of a person in your life (past or present) who this thought reminds you of or who you think taught you to think this way. When you are done writing, ask yourself what thought you want instead of this thought. In other words, who do you *want* to be, instead of what this thought is telling you you *should* be.

Example: I identify the thought, 'I shouldn't take too much for myself.' I recognize that it is the same way my grandmother thought and taught me to think. But I'm struggling with finances in life and I really need to move past this blocking belief to make better choices for myself. Choices that allow me to receive financial support and prosperity.

The problem is that if I try to let go of this thought, a fear of isolation comes up for me. That's because I feel like I'm betraying my grandmother. The result of shedding this belief would be shame and self-isolation resulting from that shame. The solution is to build up the pillar of connection and find that source of love and nourishment in myself. I do that by utilizing the strength I gained from having a powerful vision for myself, my family and my world.

Take action:

Do the 'Whose Thoughts Are These' exercise now.

Picturing your Inner Self:

Draw a picture of your inner self. Include background landscapes and other objects in the image that somehow represent that person. You can also make a list of traits if drawing isn't your thing. Do this exercise in a stream-of-consciousness kind of way – trusting your instincts.

Take action:

Do the exercise now.

MOVE

Moving your body is one of the most effective things you can do to alleviate head chatter and expedite the mental detox. A long hike or daily walk will do, but any kind of workout, dance, yoga practice or living room shuffle will help. So will making sounds, toning and kicking and punching the air.

Moving the emotion through and out of your body in this way is sure to help you open your heart again, clearing out the circling thoughts and restoring your connection with the power of your vision for yourself. Remember, what is at play here is the fear of exposing the pain in your heart. And you will have to face that pain to restore your creativity, and the silence and clarity of your mind. So, when you move your body, don't hesitate to cry, scream, laugh and otherwise shed your emotions when they come up. If you fear losing control to your emotions during these practices, allow the other pillars to support you in your expression and creation. Let them support you in clearing out the drawers in your mind so that your inner voice can move in to cohabitate and co-create with you.

Remember your pillar of receptivity and how it opens your connection to a source of love and nourishment within you. Also, remind yourself of your vision for yourself and why you are doing this healing work. But most of all, receive support. Receive it from your inner voice and any higher power you believe in. If you can, call on a friend you trust as well. Receptivity is key.

Journaling prompt:

What are your favorite ways of moving your body?

Take action:

Make a commitment to yourself to move your body in one of these ways at least once every day - for however long you are able to devote to it. 1 minute or 1 hour. When are you going to do it today?

STORIES OF MASTERS

Being alone with your mind can seem terrifying, but there are stories of masters who have been through this same journey that you can take comfort in. The stories of Buddha and Mara, Jesus in the desert, and Ezekiel's prophetic journey all have the theme of overcoming destructive mental patterns and being willing to open up to the authentic self underneath. They went though their process regardless of the unknown that it represented and regardless of the shame, temptation, and fear they had. And they became powerful, creative weavers!

These masters had to remove themselves from everything familiar and face the whirling lies chattering in their minds. They knew that to triumph, all they had to do was sit, observe, and open to the truth contained in the fertile silence deep in their heart. They did not succumb to the temptations that their inner demons put before them: The temptation to have power over others in order to feel in control, and the temptation to have magical powers in order to aggrandize themselves.

They saw through the illusion of fear and, as much as their conditioning fought to keep them imprisoned, they knew that finding out who they were at their core was more important. They knew that no matter how 'safe' it felt to stay hidden behind a wall of illusion and power, they had to shed their mental lies. They knew they would never discover their true selves without having the courage to enter into the unknown and shed the familiar. They knew these things and stayed motivated because they believed in the rightness of being who they are.

Take action:

Pick one of these stories and research it for yourself. Grab your phone right now and look it up. Write down how this story applies to you and what lessons you can use in your own practice.

CREATOR OR FORMULATOR

In the cosmology of the Kabbalah (the mystic traditions of the Jewish people), there exist four separate and inter-connected worlds. These can be viewed literally as four spiritual realms, as layers of consciousness, or they can be viewed as the process of creation - the process from inspiration to manifestation.

The first world is called Asiya (Aa-See-Ya), which translates into The World of Doing and Making. This is where you act and make things out of matter - in the physical world of which we are all a part. The second world is that of Yetzira (Yet-Zee-Ra), which translates into The World of Formation. This is the world of intellect in which you look at the visible world and *form* things out of it. It is the layer of consciousness in which you figure out *how* to do something with what you have. For example: How do I put these Legos together to make an airplane? Or, how do I put these atoms together to create a plastic molecule?

In Hebrew, the verb Yetzira (To Form) is also related to the word 'instinct.' The word for 'instinct' is Yetzer (Yet-Ser). The implication is that the world of Yetzira is also the world of base instincts rather than higher thought. It is a world where when you see something that you want you then try to possess it or achieve it. For example: You saw a boat, and you wanted one. So you *form*ulated a plan to get one. And the plan was simple. You started saving money, and when you had enough, you found a good deal on a boat and you bought it. Along the way you also studied for and got your captain's license. You followed your desire and used what you know of physical reality to get what you want.

At the consciousness level of Yetzira you are only aware of the information provided by your five senses and base desires. It is not a consciousness where you think outside the box or where you act out of a higher spiritual instinct. Yetzira and Asiya (the first two worlds) are places of reactivity where most people's consciousness live. You see something in the world, and you react with desire or with aversion. You do your best, based on your knowledge of physical reality and cultural norms, to get what you want.

The third world is the world of Beriah (Beh-Ree-Ah), which translates into The World of Creation. This is the world of new ideas and the level of consciousness where, if you had to get across a river, you would *invent* a boat, even though you had never seen one before. If you simply swam across, that would be an act of formation. But by tuning into something greater, you were able to tap into your genius and create a boat. Before making Legos that can be put together into an airplane or bond atoms into plastic, you need the idea to do so, even though no such thing existed before. In other words, you had to have the *vision* to do so, even if you didn't yet know how you were going to do it. By tapping into The World of Creation, you come up with new and innovative ideas.

A perfect example of creation comes from Henry Ford (inventor and founder of Ford Automotive). He famously said, 'If I had asked people what they wanted, they would have said, 'faster horses.'" Breeding faster horses is a perfect example of working in The World of Formation - working with the material you have in front of you. Building cars was an act of creating something completely new that came through from The World of Creation. And Henry Ford set out down that road believing in it but not knowing how he was going to accomplish it, and without any guarantee of success.

In the case of plastic, the creation vision would have been something like: How can I manipulate atoms to create a hard and yet flexible material that is also waterproof? In the case of Lego, when a child takes the pack of Legos meant to form an airplane and hides them all over the house as a treasure hunt, this is an act of creation. When the child uses them to follow the instructions and make an airplane, this is an act of formation. It is a valuable and fun learning experience, but it is not innovative. To be truly innovative, you must master both formation *and* creation.

The World of Beriah (Creation) is a world of inspirations and of greater vision. But where do the inspirations come from? They come from the fourth world of The Kabbalah, which is called Atzilut (Aat-Seal-Ut), the literal translation of which is The World of Nobility. But the literal translation does not fully describe the meaning. In Hebrew, the root of the word nobility is Etzel (Et-Sel) which means To Dwell or To Be With. The inference being that this is a realm of pure being. A place within your consciousness where everything just *is*. But *is* where? There is another hint in the word to answer that question.

The same root (Etzel) contains the word Tzel (T-sel), translating as shadow. But this is not a shadow in the sense of darkness and fear. Rather, it is a shadow in the sense of being in closest possible proximity to the divine. As Saint Hildegard of Bingen described it when talking about the source of her spiritual visions, "The Shade of the Living Light." In Jewish and Catholic theology, one cannot look at or experience the divine directly. But one can be in its shadow or shade and receive its grace.

Another way to describe the shadow of the divine experienced in The World of Nobility is as being a seed inside and under the soil. Being in the shade in the sense of being in the womb and fertile emptiness. In other words, at the place in-between the moments where you find inspiration by receiving from your inner voice. That is, if your heart is open to new experiences.

In alchemical terms this place is called *The Prima Materia* which translates to *Primal Matter* or *Primal Mother*. It is the birthplace of every process of manifestation. It is the universal, cosmic mother and giver of life which is who *you* become when you enter there. You become the mother, the feminine, the receiver (regardless of your physical gender). When in the state of consciousness of the fourth World of Nobility, the human being becomes the receptacle, the womb, and the divine inner voice functions as the spark that makes new life start to grow.

In quantum physics this is the place in which particles pop in and out of existence without apparent cause other than the effects of consciousness, because those particles *react* to your consciousness. So, when you bring your consciousness to this place of nobility and pure being, you can receive one of these particles and give it a place to grow. The particles are like little embryos waiting for a womb to hold them. And *you* are the womb.

But you don't want a random embryo implanted in your womb. To avoid that, you hold a positive intention for yourself or a question you want answered. You hold a vision. And when you hold your vision or question and enter the place in-between the moments as a receptacle, a particle pops into existence in the fertile shade of the divine. Not a random one, but one that is a direct response to the vibration you are holding (your vision or question). And by receiving the particle into yourself, you become its womb.

After receiving the answer to your question (the new particle), the information starts to make its way back down the ladder of the four worlds. In other words, the answer then gestates and grows into a coherent response. First in feeling, then as visual ideas, and then into words. When the answer proceeds through your consciousness and enters into the World of Formation, it starts to inform you *how* you are going to accomplish your vision. Which is when you take action in the World of Doing to see what the effects will be. And once you see the effect, if you need to adjust course or you have new questions to ask, you tune back into The World of Nobility. And there, in-between the moments, you receive new answers to help you course correct.

There is a saying, 'your thoughts create your reality, so make sure you put your thoughts in a place where you want to live.' This saying references that whether you are aware of it or not, a part of you is *always* connected to the Primal Matter of creation and is always receiving particles that grow and create your life from it. That is why it is of utmost importance to set a very specific intention for yourself and to make sure your heart and mind are cleared out of negative beliefs about yourself.

If you have unconscious beliefs that you are not worthy of success, your mind will receive the particles that show you how to create that unsuccessful life. The Primal Emptiness will mirror that for you and the particles will manifest as the choices you make to shape your life in that negative way. You don't want that. You don't want the negative voices in your mind creating your reality anymore.

When you master the process of intentional, positive and ever-evolving visioning, you become a true co-creator. You dwell in the place where masculine and feminine create life. When your focused vision and intention (masculine) meets your receptive feminine, together they magnetically pull the spark of life from out of the fertile emptiness. From the Prima Materia. From Chaos - Chao as the giver of life. Chaos as Sat-Chit-Ananda - The Blissful Intelligence of the Universe. The primal force from which your inspirations and creations come from and that guides you and teaches you how to formulate the materials of the world into your vision.

So, are you willing to move past your own self-judgement and fear of being who you are? Are you willing to be a full *creator* rather than a limited *formulator*? An innovator rather than just a person who looks at what they see and pieces things together based on the instruction manual that came with the box of Legos?

As a creator, you bring your fully inspired self to the conversation. You co-create with others as equals, and as people who are speaking for the inner voice, each in their own way. When you are a creator, you find your inspiration in the World of Nobility, in-between the moments. When you are closed to that part of yourself because you don't want to experience life fully, you are a formulator. A robot. A zombie. Somebody who is ruled by and manipulated by the voices of others and their base instincts.

To be a creator requires risk. It requires facing the fear of exposure and possibly of rejection and isolation. It also requires you to receive love and inspiration from a higher consciousness. And if you believe you don't deserve that love, you won't allow inspiration in. Inspiration - the word itself means to receive your own spirit. And your spirit is *full* of love. It is *made* of love. Receive it and allow it to transform you.

And if you feel vulnerable? That's great! Because vulnerability means you are about to tap into a layer of genius in yourself, and that your inner demons are trying to keep you tied to a lower-world existence. Vulnerability is what you experience when you approach the doubt in yourself. It is what you feel when your self-judgement kicks in and you fear retaliation or humiliation for being who you are.

These are the illusory walls keeping you out of your castle. So, when you feel that vulnerability, let it be a sign you are on the right track, about to embody power from your pillar of connection and walk right through the walls. Take it as a sign that you are about to kick your demons out and move on with your life without looking back, moving on to a place where there is only you, your inner voice, and the rightness of being who you are.

When you dispel the illusory walls keeping you from your castle, your creator consciousness will rise from within and blossom. You will free your heart in service to your own evolution and the evolution of your vision for yourself and the world 10,000 years from now that you are right now co-creating with everybody else. And the more people choose a good future, the sooner that future will happen. Who knows... maybe even within your lifetime.

Journaling prompts:

1. Are you willing to fully embrace being a creator rather than just a formulator?

2. Write about the difference between formulator and creator as it applies to your own life. Where have you been a formulator? When have you been a creator?

3. Describe what kind of creator you want to be.

4. What are the primary negative thoughts that try to stop you from being a creator?

5. Look back at your journaling notes and write a new vision statement. One that includes your commitment to be a co-creator and what your highest intention for yourself and the world is going to be.

Take action:

Put your new vision up on your wall. Add images to it in order to give it more life.

A WALL OF DISRUPTIVE THOUGHTS

There is a teaching from the Buddhist tradition that goes like this: When you walk barefoot, you might cut your feet. The solution isn't to smooth out the surfaces of the entire world, but rather to put shoes on your own feet.

As we have seen, one reason the fear of exposure might surface for you is the amount of difficulty there is in the world and the amount of real or fictional violence you are exposed to. It is natural to be afraid of the world and the many dangers it contains. And on some level, you may want to eliminate all those dangers. Your fear of exposure may even perpetuate your wall of disruptive thoughts by trying to solve all the problems of the world and by trying to read everybody's thoughts so you can please them. And yet, you can't solve all the problems of the world, and you certainly won't be able to please everybody all the time.

The reality is that the world is dangerous. But you don't have to feel like you are in danger. The solution is not in finding a way to take all dangers out of the world but rather to have faith in your own inner voice, knowing it will never betray you (even if the results you get when following it are not what you expected). You can be a person who leads by example and who, through faith in yourself, creatively weaves their light into the world. In small ways at first, and then in bigger ways. Wearing your inner voice like sandals that protect you from harm.

As long as you keep trying to change things you have no control over, you will continue being a formulator. A person who reacts, not creates. And you will miss opportunities to make a real difference in people's lives in the here and now. The present is when you are needed, not the past or the future. Right here is where you are wanted, not in the news from the other side of the world. Your heart belongs in your daily reality, not watching Game of Thrones. A game where horrible things happen to good people and you can't do anything about it.

To truly make a difference in the world, we each have to take responsibility and focus first on what we have control over within ourselves. What do you have control over within yourself? Can you be in integrity? Can you be authentic regardless of consequence? Can you model that for the world around you? For the ones you love?

Journaling prompts:
1. Can you be in integrity?
2. Can you be authentic regardless of consequence and model that for the world around you?
3. What do you have control over within yourself that you haven't allowed yourself to admit you have control over?

Example: I have control over the way I express myself when I'm feeling grumpy. Up until now, I've pretended like that place in me is not under my control and that it was just my 'emotional expression.' But the truth is that I can choose to change that.

AUTHENTIC PEOPLE

Allowing your inner voice to rise up and scatter the crusty thoughts that keep your heart frozen is where you begin building your pillar of creativity. This is the only way you will ever help make real change in your world. On a small scale, starting with yourself first. You can be who you really are and you can find the people who will support you in that. There is no doubt! There is only the rightness of being who you really are and the unique weaving of creativity that you are capable of bringing into the world through an open heart.

Opening your heart is the work of the true mystic. It is a deep, non-verbal experience that is powered by your vision, your receptivity to your inner voice and your faith in the rightness of being who you are. It is not something you can do on your own. It is something you have to let the artist within you - the inner voice - the sculptor living in The World of Nobility do for you. Going through the trials to uncover the silence in your heart will make a positive impact on the world, on yourself, and on your family for generations to come. More of an impact than you can ever imagine. Authentic people (whether their lives ended in triumph or tragedy) are remembered and looked up to as role models and heroes.

Every person on the path of awakening must face their demons eventually. And no matter how afraid you are of them, staying rooted in the rightness of being who you are will act as a break-wave to the onslaught and as a lighthouse to those around you. It will fill your heart with grace and gratitude, allowing the flames of creativity to come bursting forward to be, live, and create something more beautiful than you could ever imagine.

Journaling Prompt:

Who are the people you know or have met that you believe have a strong pillar of creativity. What can you learn from them?

Take action:

Ask the people you know who have a strong pillar of creativity for advice on building yours. Reach out to at least one person right now. Journal about the advice they give.

Journaling prompt:

Make something beautiful: Make some art, write a poem, dance, or otherwise create something to represent your open heart.

Example:

Shine, Feel

I am

In my heart of hearts true

To my own nature.

I hunt, I gather, I speak.

Not when spoken to but when my voice

Raises the dead. The depressed. The anxious.

To all of you I speak. Never stop.

Be alive. Be natural.

Reach out in unspoken verse

And touch another. Connect. Create.

Love. Nourish. Shine. Feel.

~ Aaran Solh

Your turn… Make something beautiful!

THE UPWARD SPIRAL

The four pillars do not stand alone. They build on each other and create an upward moving spiral. Picture this: four short pillars and a roof. As you build up one pillar, your roof becomes lopsided. You must build up your other pillars to match before you can build the first one higher again. Each time you build a pillar higher, you need to put effort into the others to match.

THE UPWARD SPIRAL OF VISION

Without a strong vision, you will never have the strength to endure the trials of creation. The inevitable rejections, the setbacks, the failures. You won't be able to endure facing the pain in your own heart, under which your creativity is buried. You need to believe in your vision to help keep you going and bust free of your cage. If you don't, you will give up and you will hide away in the familiar and never show the world your true colors.

And when you are creating your vision, if you don't learn how to be receptive and learn how to trust your communication with your inner voice, you will never create one that motivates you and stretches you so much that you believe it's worth fighting for. A vision that cuts through the illusions of doubt and lights a fire at your core that won't ever go out. One that turns water into the steam that fuels your engine.

Your vision won't grow deeper and more solid if you can't be receptive enough to the knowledge you need to attain it. Or receptive to the people who unexpectedly come into your life offering to take you somewhere and help you. Without trusting those people, your ability to connect won't grow and your ability to bring passion from within you to every moment because you feel supported on the inside won't grow either.

Building your vision and passion requires action. Without a solid connection to a spiritual source of nourishment and love within, you won't have the courage to face the inevitable consequences that taking action in a new direction will bring, often leading to major changes in your life. The kinds of changes that are hard to cope with without knowing you are held by a spiritual source within. You must be able to find nourishment in your relationship with your inner voice or your vision will wither like an untended flower in a pot as you fall prey to the nay-sayers in your life and in your head.

You must be able to believe in your vision alone. You have to believe in it in the dark and when the world rejects you and tells you that you are not good enough. And you have to open your heart to the pain you have experienced in life and convert it into fuel to create more and more of your vision. Without an open heart, your vision won't be honest. It won't be real. It won't be raw and it won't have fire. And creation without fire is incredibly dull. It's like earth without heat. You end up with a barren, frozen rock. Creation without deep, direct truth doesn't interest or inspire anybody. Creation without receptivity to (and action taken on) the intuitions that come to you is shallow, unremarkable and boring.

Journaling prompt:

How are you going to utilize the 3 pillars of connection, receptivity and creativity to build your pillar of vision?

THE UPWARD SPIRAL OF CONNECTION

Ultimately, there is only one source of nourishment and connection, though in your meditations it can take many shapes and forms to make you feel nourished, safe and loved. And how do you connect to this elusive source of all? By knowing that this source is the collective consciousness of all humanity and that you share a common core vision with it, and with everyone. That vision is a desire for peace, freedom and connection. Not one person exists who doesn't want these things, though so many of us our misguided in our search. It's easy enough to close your eyes and feel that.

Close your eyes, take a few deep breaths and feel how at our core, we all desire peace, freedom, and connection.

No matter how the gifts of your inner voice shine through your particular prism, you can give your gift with an underlying desire to create peace, freedom and connection for everybody. And by having an underlying collectivist motivation for your work, your experience of connection will grow so much more than doing your work for selfish purposes. Though, by all means, be selfish. Pursue prosperity, health and pleasure for yourself and your family. Just do it with an underlying desire to make everything better for everybody. It's the fertilizer that makes your own tree grow faster. When you receive selfishly from a place of wanting to serve wholeheartedly, you build your pillars by creating an upward spiral.

People have a natural inclination to connect and give. And yet, there is an important part of giving that is often overlooked. And that is, being able to receive. After all, if we all started giving, but no one was receiving, we'd find ourselves in a bit of trouble. To be in real connection, you need to be both a giver and a receiver. Without receiving strength and vision from your inner voice and from others around you, you might not have the courage to open your heart to your own pain. And if you can't open your heart, your ability to feel will be hampered and you won't ever truly be able to give to others.

Truly giving and receiving with another person allows you to *feel* each other. To have an intuitive non-verbal experience of unity. Feeling each other reminds you of your mutual source. The source as it is witnessed and reflected through another unique soul. It reminds you of the nourishment within you.

This is the beauty of relationship. Relationship gives you a vision of what it is possible to attain within *yourself*. When you can feel and connect with another person, you see a reflection of the source of nourishment within. The mistake most people make, however, is to then expect the vast unconditional source to come through that other person and be nourished by it, expecting the other to be the 'all'.

This mistake is the number one destroyer of relationship. Instead, treat relationship (both with your inner voice and with others) as a spiral as well (or maybe a see-saw). When you deepen into feeling another person, you need to take a break, pull back, and deepen equally into yourself. Then you can come back to the other with more and more gifts and enrichment from within you. In the same vein, when you deepen into your inner voice and connect, you can then take action in the world and discover where that takes you. After doing that, you can turn back in and go deeper with new questions and receive new paradigms.

As you receive the reflection of the source through another (a person or a spiritual being), you can use that feeling of external connection as a stepping stone to bring you closer to that source of love and nourishment within yourself. And when you start to do that naturally, your creativity and your ability to confidently follow your inner voice strengthen, and of course, your own experience of peace, freedom, and connection grow as well.

Journaling prompt:

How are you going to utilize the 3 pillars of vision, receptivity and creativity to build your pillar of connection?

THE UPWARD SPIRAL OF RECEPTIVITY

You can't do anything alone. You must learn how to receive and co-create with your inner voice and others in your world. Accepting every reaction to your creations as constructive, supportive feedback for re-direction (rather than with resentment) is, to say the least, helpful to your peace of mind and projects. Learning to be accepting in this way requires a confidence that comes from an internal connection to a source of love within you. If you don't have that, everything will come across as criticism and shaming and you will give up after your first round of setbacks (and there will be many).

Since there will be many, let's consider what a setback is. A setback is really just another word for disillusionment. And, yes, people tend to think of disillusionment as a bad thing. But think about it. Getting rid of illusions is actually a good goal to have. It helps you to better see what you need for your creativity to grow or your projects move forward. When you receive knowledge, you receive disillusionment. When you receive support, it's possible you become disillusioned with yourself, potentially shedding the illusion that you are a super-human do-it-all-your-self-er. It's really not a bad thing.

Consider this: No one has ever written a masterpiece without writing a terrible first-draft. No master artist ever painted a cathedral wall without spending a year sketching and burning drafts. Only those creators with the ability to confidently receive feedback and course-corrections succeed in the end. And yes, you are a creator in whatever arena you choose to express yourself.

You must learn to trust that every turn of events is leading you to your destination even if it feels like rejection or the events appear so incredibly different from what you expected or what you want them to look like. Around every turn in the road you must shed your original assumptions about what is supposed to be there. Otherwise, you end up pushing blindly against the prison wall of expectations, trying to make reality into something it isn't instead of receiving reality for what it is and working from there.

In the current world culture of capitalism and competition you have to earn your right to succeed and shine. And while it is unfortunate that we have not yet created a world of conscious equals, there is an opportunity here to help you grow. Like the butterfly pushing out of its cocoon to strengthen its wings you must do the daily work and trust the light when you are in complete darkness. No one can do it for you or your wings won't be strong enough to make you fly. Every day you need to remember to feel the pain of the billions of people who are lost and of a planet on the verge of death. Feel that. And know that there are others like you who have a vision of the paradise it can be *re*-turned into.

Stop and feel the pain. And stop to feel your community of visionaries around you. Let this fuel your vision.

Your invisible community doesn't know how things are going to unfold. But they open their hearts in vulnerability just as you have and they hold a vision. They are receptive to the inner voice that shows them which way to go and when they hear that voice, no matter how frightened they are, they follow it. Because they know that if they don't, their heart will shut down and their creativity will die.

And if you stray? Just know that no matter how many times you stray, you can always go back. The path is always there for you to walk. No matter how many times you fall asleep, you can wake up again. With the support of millions of others who want the same thing as you. People who want to live peacefully in a world of harmony where we all take care of each other. Where we all know that the inner voice that speaks through you is the same inner voice that speaks through me. Where we know we are extensions of the same source. Where we know that we can touch each other in our minds and form a collective that cannot be stopped.

Hold to your vision of a greater world. Hold to it and reach out within yourself to all the people out there who share it. Call to them to support you and offer your support in return. You can do it. We all can. Please don't ever stop. Receive us all into your heart. And let that support create an upward spiral of love, sourced from the connection within you to the source of all.

Journaling prompt:
How are you going to utilize the 3 pillars of vision, connection and creativity to build your pillar of receptivity?

THE UPWARD SPIRAL OF CREATIVITY

Your creativity can't grow unless you allow your ability to connect to love, nourishment and support grow. Without being internally connected to love, you won't find the power to heal old wounds and open your heart to the pleasures as well as to the pains of life. You must cultivate a strong experience of connection or your strength and ability to truly feel will fade, and with it, your creativity. Because your creations arise from the silence in your heart when it is open to feeling. But to feel in this way, connection isn't enough, you also need a powerful vision. Without vision, you will never be motivated enough to endure what you feel. Without vision, you won't have a strong enough need. And while the power to heal comes from your internal pillar of connection, the power and drive to endure the healing comes from your vision.

Without the pillar of receptivity, you will never make space in your life for those times when your heart needs attention. When you just need to stop and feel, and cry tears of joy, pain, letting go, or relief. You will never really stop to appreciate the miracles in your life. Without receptivity, you will never fully understand that creativity flows when it has time and a safe place. You must be receptive to support and trust the perfect timing of your creation coming into being. Because really, what choice do you have? Your heart is not something that can be rushed. Your heart is the pacemaker of your soul. Receive it's wisdom and trust the timing will be perfect.

But be careful - because without a passionate vision, giving your heart time to feel can also become an excuse to procrastinate. To avoid this trap, remember - there is nothing more powerful than clear action taken in the direction you want your life to go in, no matter how small or even symbolic the action is, and even if your creativity isn't fully flowing. It's an upward spiral. Take a small action, feel everything that comes up for you around that and the momentum will start to open your heart more and more to your natural creativity.

And, of course, don't forget to be receptive to support, both in the form of inspiration from within and from other people in your community. It's clear - without receptivity, you will never be strong enough to create or open to the knowledge of *how* to create (what action to take towards your vision). You will also never be able to find the inner strength needed to push the boulder of your vision up the hill and attain your creation.

If you can't receive spaciousness into your life and trust the organic timing of the universe, you will exhaust yourself trying to push against a rock that's still halfway buried in the earth. If you are constantly racing the clock, you will miss the cues and the signposts (not to mention the view) and you will never relax enough to enjoy the ride. And if you don't enjoy the ride, you will never be able to teach others to enjoy *their* ride and you will never help create something that actually nourishes the world, because if you are not nourished, you can't create something nourishing.

If you are not receptive and trusting, you can't create a community of co-creative, safe and reliable adults with vision. A community that can create a movement that changes the world as we know it. Or changes your neighborhood. Or changes your family life. Or changes your own ability to be happy. If your heart won't trust and receive, you can't connect, and you can't deepen into your vision. And if you can't deepen into your vision, you can't create.

When your heart can trust and receive in this way, your creativity can flow honestly and with pure emotion. The kind of emotion that inspires others. Not the timid whispers that come from a heart that won't feel or take a stand. When your creation is informed by your ability to feel, that's when you make other people feel. When you do things 'your way,' that's when you become an empathic leader. When you try to connect solely from an intellectual understanding of something, people call bullshit faster than they can press the 'back' button on their browser.

Real connection to other people can only take place when your heart is open to feeling them. And when your mind isn't getting lost in your fears about what they think. Or feeling guilty about how terrible your own confidence and openness might make *them* feel. When you create from a place of strong vision, your art says something. And it says something important. It creates dialogue. Maybe even controversy. It moves people to act and it moves them out of their unmotivated slumber. It inspires.

Without an experience of connection within yourself, you will be too afraid of creating in this way. And without a vision for yourself (even a small one), you probably won't take action. So if you are stuck, you should take action no matter how faltering or doubtful the action is. And no matter how many mistakes you make (or think you are going to make). It is only by taking action that you will fine tune your vision and begin to comprehend the long-term pathway to attaining it through your open and creative heart.

Journaling prompt:

How are you going to utilize the 3 pillars of vision, connection and receptivity to build your pillar of creativity?

KEEP MOVING

The pillars each build on and support each other. When you get stuck building one, it's because you need to work on a different one for now before you can keep building the current one. So always ask yourself, 'which pillar do I need to work on today?' Then ask your inner voice how to do that work. Also utilize the self-diagnosis tool in the appendix.

Just because you learn to be receptive, creative, connected and have vision doesn't mean you enter into a 'done for you' deal. You are still a co-creator. You still need to do your part day in and day out in order to contribute to the relationship. You still need to be brave and determined enough to burn through your pain and to be alive to the pain of the world. To be alive in this way is to squeeze the true juice of your creativity from that place where it is born - the stillness and vast potential of your open heart.

If you don't show up for your marriage, neither will your partner. If you don't show up at work, you will get fired. If you don't put in the time, effort and bravery, you won't get the full attention of your inner voice and you won't know which way to turn next time you are at a crossroads. And instead of your inner voice guiding you, the voice of your second-grade teacher who made you stand in the corner in shame for moving around too much will. Or the voice of the bully will, telling you to run and hide so you don't get picked on.

You are either building or you are decaying. There is no such thing as immobility in this life (even though it feels that way sometimes). If you are not active in building your pillars, you are allowing them to fall apart and with them your dreams of fulfilling your life purpose and creating something good for the world out of your unique gifts.

Intuition is about so much more than getting clear answers to life's questions from your inner voice. It is ultimately about awakening to the truth of yourself. It's about being present in the moment. Or rather, in-between the moments. It's about allowing yourself to be guided by something greater than yourself, and then finally, coming to the realization that that something *is* you.

Having clear and consistent intuition simply means you are seeing the truth. And as you build your pillars, you will start to feel more aligned with truth than you ever have been. You will start hearing and seeing things in new ways. There will be new layers of information that open to you when you are in conversation. You will start to find that truths that are self evident to you, are completely unknown to others. So much so, that you might find yourself wondering if you need to find new people to talk to.

That's all okay. It's all normal. It's all part of the process of awakening to your true self. But it takes time to get there. At this junction, the most important thing for you to do is open to the guidance of your inner voice by building the 4 pillars of intuition. Wanting more from life than what you have had so far is the first step on a truly courageous journey. Allowing your inner voice to guide you on that journey - to be your navigator - is the next step.

Remember the Rumi quote at the beginning of this book? "When you look for God, God is in the look of your eyes. In the thought of looking. Nearer to you than yourself." Nearer to you than yourself… That's the true source of intuition. That is the moment between the moments. The moment when you become aware that The Blissful Intelligence of the Universe is looking through your eyes in complete and silent knowing. The moment when the question and the answer arise simultaneously.

Rumi has another quote, "Out beyond right-doing and wrong-doing there is a field, I'll meet you there." If you really want to get to that place, the most important thing you can do is practice. And your practice time is simply the time you dedicate to building your relationship to your inner voice. To truth.

So, make sure you utilize all the tools at your disposal. Download the companion meditations to this book from the website and practice them regularly. Don't stop just because you have reached the end of the book. Let the practices and community that is available to you help you build up your pillars layer upon layer in an upward moving spiral until you reach that point of silent understanding. Where there is only a meeting, never a seeking.

And if you still find yourself struggling with discipline. I've got news for you…

DISCIPLINE DOESN'T EXIST

THE AGE OF UN-REASON

Hope and faith have fallen from grace along with the major religions of the world. You might say they are collateral damage to intellectualism and the mass rejection of patriarchy and abuse associated with some churches, cults, and even yoga studios. The rejection is so massive that even those who dare to go beyond religion into becoming true mystics are eyed uneasily by many people and put in a category of nutters and scam artists. If, in Western culture, you offer yourself in devotion to something greater than yourself and that something talks back to you, you might even be referred to a psychiatrist and offered a prescription to help you get over it.

At the same time as hope and faith have become the purview of nutters, discipline has taken a back seat to the fetishes of comfort, apathy, helplessness, and denial, especially discipline associated with spiritual practice. This is not only because of the mass rejection of it in the mainstream but also because of not knowing who to trust as a teacher. Like any subject you want to learn, when you approach the topic of spirituality (call it intuition, meditation, personal-growth, or anything else), you would first seek out a teacher. But there are many teachers from many traditions and the teachings are disjointed. There is no clear go-to authority like in the old days and there is no system in place for you to follow - no mystery school, village shaman, or trustworthy clergy to turn to outside your local new-age bookstore where you may find initial support, but only rarely, long term, in-depth programs for transformation.

In this age of disjointed spiritual teachings and abusive priests and gurus, it is easy to lose hope that there is an authentic spirituality to turn to. The true gift of this age though, is that each of us is offered the opportunity to find our own voice, trust it and follow it. If you don't choose to have faith in that, you die off as a relic of an age past, controlled by others until your energy is finally drained and you are disposed of unceremoniously with a retirement check (if you are lucky) and poor medical care.

If you find that you wake up in the morning, hit the snooze button, and go back to sleep and later in the day grumble about your lack of discipline, you have missed a very important point. *There is no such thing as discipline!* Discipline is choice. It is a choice to be happy. You either choose to follow your inner voice and be happy as a result or you choose to appease depression, numbness, and apathy and be unfulfilled for the rest of your life. If you need something to prompt you to action, perhaps you only need to contemplate that.

Don't want to live the rest of your life in this way? Inquire within yourself: 'What do I know to be true in my heart? Is there meaning in creating something positive for myself, my neighbors, and the world, or is there only an endless dark night where life is misery; and disease, suffering, and death inevitably come for everybody so there is no point in doing anything?' Don't try to answer in words. Feel the answer non-verbally in your body.

Take action:

Stop and feel the answer right now, without trying to make sense of it. Describe your experience.

FAITH

If you can't feel the answer to the question above or don't have faith in your own experience of it, your focus every minute of every day must be to find that answer. Every practice you do and every question you ask of your inner voice must be to help you see that there is meaning in working hard and in leaving your comfort zone, even as it puts your very identity at risk, and even if it causes you financial, emotional or physical difficulty (by leaving your job, your relationship, taking a stand on a topic that is controversial, etc.). You must build your faith in your own experience with all your might, heart and soul knowing there is meaning in what you do (even if you don't know what that meaning is in yet) or you will never do anything.

Growing up in Western culture, you may be so conditioned to only follow what you can *comprehend* that you completely ignore the messages from your inner voice, expecting logic and logistics to build you a bridge where only faith in your own non-verbal experience can. There is a powerful verse in the New Testament (John 1:5): 'And the Light shineth in the darkness, and the darkness comprehended it not.' What this means in our context is that even though you can feel the Light (or your inner voice) in your heart, you most assuredly will not comprehend it intellectually. It is, in fact, beyond your ability to comprehend and if you try too hard to make sense of it, you will lose touch with the feeling of it and your faith that it will guide you to something meaningful will dwindle back into the shadows of your unconscious.

You must have faith in the *experience* of your inner voice even though that experience can never be expressed in words, and even though having this kind of faith isn't widely embraced in Western culture. You must choose to rise out of the collective slumber and be different, even though people around you may be depressed and drugged to the point of apathy. You must rise up even if it requires you to leave the safety of your own home; figuratively, in your mind, for certain, or even literally travel to a faraway land like Abraham, Jesus, and Buddha did, and like many people traveling on a path of spiritual exploration have.

Every spiritual journey inevitably comes to this point, where you are standing at the edge of the abyss beyond your intellect (the borderland) and there is no visible way to cross it. This point in the journey is called *the leap of faith*. Not faith in the sense of believing what somebody else tells you, but faith in your own non-verbal experience and inner voice, and following what you know to be true in your heart. It is often called *blind faith,* because you are asked to trust in something you can't see. It is not, however, something you can't feel. The abyss you come to on the spiritual journey is dark because you must close your eyes (your intellect) to see what is in it. You must close your eyes and *feel.*

Take action:

Close the eyes of your intellect and open the eyes of feeling. What do you experience?

HOPE *IS* DISCIPLINE

Even if you develop faith in your inner voice, you might still get overwhelmed with negative thinking and give up, so what should you do? First, it's important to get clear on the real question. Many people beat themselves up for not being 'disciplined' in their practice or the pursuit of their dreams but few stop to ask themselves what they actually mean by 'discipline,' and the answer is simple. Discipline, as we said above, is choice, but like any choice, making it, is the result of circumstances that come together to prompt you to action. Discipline is not something you *have,* it is action that takes place organically when (1) you have hope that a positive outcome exists. And (2) hope that it is possible for you to attain it. So, if you have faith in your inner voice but still lack what you call 'discipline,' you have either:

1. **Lost hope that a positive outcome exists because…**
   - It's too much work
   - You can't do it alone
   - There is too much to fight against
   - You think you don't deserve it
   - Any other 'I can't' statement you find in your mind…
2. **Lost hope that your desired outcome can be achieved because…**
   - Things will just fall apart
   - You might lose what you already have if you try
   - You will never be happy anyway

- There is no justice in the world
- Any other negative interpretation of the world that keeps you safe from having to risk failure and rejection.

If you don't have hope, there is no reason to act or to *be disciplined,* as it were. When you have hope, you can't help but care, and when you care, you are driven to action by a primal emotion, even if that action is difficult or seems dangerous. If your child was about to be hit by a truck, you would run into the street. Not because you knew the truck wouldn't end up hitting both of you, but because you had hope that it would not (you could see the possible positive outcome) and you hoped you would succeed in saving your child (you thought you might be able to do it). You cared more about the possible outcome than you cared about the danger.

To have discipline in your practice, you must feel the same hope about building a relationship with your inner voice and following its guidance: Because you know that down any other path there is only misery and that if you don't follow that voice, you will end up as devastated as if that truck hit your child. Hopefully by this point, you have come to know that you deserve better than misery and understand that love, nourishment, and knowledge are readily available to you once you have learned to receive them, no matter how conditioned you were to think of yourself as undeserving.

All the information and exercises in this book are meant to help you see the possible positive outcomes you can help create and to help you see that it is possible for you to achieve them - to show you there is good reason to have hope. You know what they say though: 'you can lead a horse to water but you can't make it drink.' This book has led you to water, but it is up to you to drink it. In other words, this book can't make you jump in front of that truck to save your (inner) child, only your hope will make you do that.

Whenever you find you lack discipline, ask yourself, 'What choice am I making for myself right now? A choice to have hope in a positive outcome and faith that my inner voice will lead me there, or the choice to keep myself safe from possible failure and rejection?' When you ask yourself that question, take a deep breath, remind yourself of your motivation and your vision for the world, connect to a source of love within you and receive the answer. Use the Borderland Meditation to help you.

Once you have made your choice, ask your inner voice, 'right now, this second, what can I do to be happy and fulfill my potential in this world?' You can, of course, change the ending of that question to anything you choose. The most important part of asking the question being that you act on the answer you get. Discipline is a leap of faith, and that leap of faith is action, even if that means the answer in the moment is to meditate with a clear question or intention, or a prayer of gratitude. Whatever it is, follow it.

At the risk of sounding like a broken record: You can build your hope and faith by practicing regularly and by spending time with your inner voice and building that relationship, and when you hear it whispering, follow it. Do it in small ways at first and then bigger and bigger ones as your faith in the unseen grows, creating an upward spiral of momentum. Devoting time to that relationship through practice is the only way it will grow and if you find you need a structured system to help you stay on track, you can use the Awakening to the Mystic Meditations found on the website:

www.AwakeningMystic.com

Take action:

Make a choice to have hope in a positive outcome and have faith that your inner voice will lead you there. Now act on that faith.

AFTERWARD

Congratulations on Completing Empath to Mystic!

A few end notes:

My hope is that you took the time to do the practices and have created a true opening in your heart for your authentic self. Training yourself to continuously look to your inner voice for guidance is, like anything else, a matter of putting in the time and effort. The payoff is enormous and everybody around you will benefit from the effort, so it is worth putting in the time. If you haven't yet, please take a moment to browse the appendices of the book, I believe that the daily practices as well as the self-diagnosis tool will be most valuable.

1. If you want to learn to be a carpenter, you need two things: you need a workshop and you need to go into that workshop, cut wood, and glue it together. If you want to master your intuition and be a mystic you need a place to practice and you need to practice. If you haven't yet, dedicate a corner of a room in your home and build a small alter. If you can, and have the privilege, dedicate a whole room to it. The greater presence you give to this work in your life, the greater presence it will have! When you do your Empath to Mystic practices, or any other personal or spiritual growth work, use that space. The more you use it, the more it becomes natural and feels like home to you.

2. Now that you have completed this book, don't put it on a shelf to collect dust. Go back to the beginning and start over. Remember, building your pillars is an upward spiral, so the information will take you to new places now that *you* are in a new place. If you don't want to read the whole book cover to cover again, you can skim through the book and see what catches your eye. Trust your intuition about it, and read that section again or do that practice or journaling prompt again. Additionally, you can use this book like a tarot card deck. When you are feeling a lack of inspiration, sit for a moment, focus on your question and then open the book where you feel guided - find out what your inner voice wants you to know.

3. Finally, as an author, I highly appreciate the feedback I get from my readers. If you enjoyed this book, please consider leaving a short review on Amazon.com. It will help others make an informed decision before buying my book. And don't forget to visit my website to access free supplementary material such as guided meditations, videos, and journaling worksheets: www.AaranSolh.com

4. If you haven't yet discovered The Awakening To The Mystic spiritual growth program that takes your work in this book to the next level, please look it up at: www.AwakeningMystic.com.

Thank you and with love,
Aaran Solh

APPENDIX I: SELF DIAGNOSIS

There are two ways for you to diagnose which pillar needs maintenance right now. Simply answer the two questions below, and if you find your answers to the two questions are different, please take it as a sign to look at both pillars.

When you complete your diagnosis, refer to the next appendix, Pillar Practices, for solutions. Also look within the relevant chapters at the actions steps and journaling prompts. If you haven't yet, please visit www.AaranSolh.com where you can join the Inner Circle and download free guided meditations and worksheets organized by pillar.

The Challenge Test

Answer this question: What is currently (in this moment) my greatest challenge when it comes to following my inner voice?

1. I have too much head-chatter.
2. I allow other people's doubts and judgements to influence me.
3. I don't have enough discipline, motivation or structure.
4. I have too many activities and obligations to take time for it.

1. **I have too much head chatter: Work on your pillar of creativity**. Focus your attention on opening your heart. Find the feelings and old pains that are blocking you from truly experiencing life. Release them to find the silence within and allow your inspiration to organically flow from there.

2. **I allow other people's doubts and judgements to influence me: Work on your pillar of connection.** Focus on building your internal connection to a source of spiritual love and nourishment. Remind yourself that you can't please everybody and that you never will. Remind yourself that love and authenticity heal even if love has to tear down structures and relationships in your life that are based on lies.

3. **I don't have enough discipline, motivation or structure: Work on your pillar of vision.** You need to remember why you are on this path. Ask yourself: What good can come out of my actions? What meaning can I bring to people's

lives? What can I bring to my own life? What simple action can I take right now, this second, towards that vision? No matter how small it is, act today, evaluate what you learned from it, and then take another action.

4. **I have too many activities and obligations to take time for it: Work on your pillar of receptivity.** Take a moment to rest and open to the natural flow, in-between the moments. Enter a space of timelessness and spaciousness and take a few seconds to receive. On a practical level, ask yourself if you are saying 'yes' to things you really want to be saying 'no' to. Also ask yourself, 'who can I turn to for support and advice (both internally and externally)?

The Emotion Test

This test is a little bit more subtle. If you can't answer the question right away, take a few deep breaths and tune in to the emotions under the surface.

Answer this question: What are the primary negative emotions currently (in this moment) occupying my mind (choose the closest one)? I am feeling…

1. Angry and resentful
2. Depressed and sad
3. Numb and stuck
4. Helpless or out-of-control

1. **Angry and resentful: Work on your pillar of vision.** Resentment often comes up when you don't believe there is a way out - when you feel oppressed. You must have a vision that propels you forward. A vision that allows you to believe that there's a better way for everybody in this world to be.

2. **Depressed or sad: Work on your pillar of connection.** Sadness often arises when you are telling yourself over and over 'I can't'. Or rather, when other people tell you that you can't and you believe them. Take stock of those voices in your head that are telling you that you 'can't.' Reconnect to a positive source of love and nourishment in the spiritual realms.

3. **Numb and Stuck: Work on your pillar of creativity.** Feeling numb often accompanies a heart that is closed and therefore unable to feel. Start by asking yourself what emotion or pain is underneath the numbness. If it's too much to deal with, seek out help. But also, take creative action. Even if it's just to doodle, dance, or make music. Creating releases the flow of energy. Also, take some time to unplug and walk in the woods, reconnecting to the natural world.

4. **Helpless or out-of-control: Work on your pillar of receptivity.** Feeling out of control usually happens because you are trying to control everything (and guess

what - you can't). You may be trying to shape the world according to your vision. And that's wonderful, but you are missing something. You are missing your co-pilot. Remember to turn to your inner voice to receive guidance and support and to make sure that you only say 'yes' when it's time to say 'yes,' and that you say 'no,' when, for you, it's clearly time to say 'no.'

APPENDIX II: PILLAR PRACTICES

In this appendix, you will find lists of practices divided by the pillar they help build and support. On the author's website, you will find additional videos, guided meditations, and worksheets specifically designed to support the building of the pillars. Please don't hesitate to utilize them as well. www.AaranSolh.com

For building your pillar of vision

1. Write down at least 4 ways you know you can serve other people. For example: Volunteering at a shelter, listening to someone who is in need, knitting a sweater, or organizing your friend's stamp collection. This list can be made up of anything - anything at all. Once you have made your list, choose one item, and act on it today - make somebody's life better.

2. Choose one single goal that you have - big or small. Break it down into the smallest possible steps to achieving it. For example: I want to go to the gym today. Step 1: Open my calendar. Step 2: Choose a time. Step 3: Pack a gym bag. Step 4: Remember to take it with me. Step 5: Ask a friend to hold me accountable so I don't chicken out. Step 6: Etc… And then of course, follow through.

3. Take an action that scares you - something you have been putting off for fear of failure. Have a conversation you have been postponing. Do something new. Have an adventure. Break up your routine. Anything to put you in a new environment that can help you find inspiration.

4. Ask yourself what pain is alive in you today. Is something old coming up for you from childhood? Did you watch something on the news that made you angry? What is making you feel bad today? Define it clearly and then remind yourself that you are alive so that you can do something about that pain, and so other people don't have to suffer that same pain. Find others who care about the same issues or find an organization you can contribute to that has the same principles as you.

5. Is your vision too hard for you to believe in? Adjust your vision to be something you can believe in with your whole heart. Something completely attainable, even if it's not your final or grand vision.

6. Do something competitive, even if it's just racing your kids down the street or playing chess with somebody in the park.

For building your pillar of connection

1. Call up a non-verbal experience of feeling safe, nourished and loved in your body. You don't have to have a visual recollection of when and where you felt this way, simply recall the feeling in your body. When you have even the smallest experience of that feeling accessible, allow that feeling to spread and bring relaxation to your entire body. You will be surprised how much tension this exercise releases.

2. Do the 'Whose Thoughts Are These Anyway' exercise. In one column write down the self-sabotaging thoughts you are having and in the next write down where and from whom you got those thoughts. Once you have several down on paper, go through each and speak it out loud and then say to yourself, 'I don't have to think this way anymore. Instead I choose to think…'

3. Ask yourself, 'Who am I serving by making myself small? Who are the people in my life that I think will have to adapt if I start to speak up more, and who might be challenged if I start to be more myself than I ever have been?' Write down what you'd like to say to those people.

4. Take yourself out for dinner and a movie, go for a walk by yourself or anything else you consider fun (by yourself).

5. What memories of isolation and rejection are coming up for you right now? How are you afraid those experiences are going to repeat in your life today? Do some writing, create some art or dance in your living room to express these emotions.

6. Notice if within you there is a statement such as: 'If only I could be there… or attain that… everything would be ok.' Notice how it's really the feeling of home, safety, love, respect and support that you are craving. Let yourself be in relationship with that feeling in the here and now. Invite it to you and allow it to transform you. Build a relationship with it without expectations of what that will look like.

7. Stand in a place where you can be alone. Put on some music you feel intuitively related to in the moment. Think about what you want in your life. Feel those parts within you that are saying 'I can't' to it. Find the resistance in your body and begin to dance. Through the dance, allow your body to unravel the energetic knots of resistance. As you become aware of the thoughts and feelings that create your resistance, make sounds and movements that help you expel them from your body.

For building your pillar of receptivity

1. Stop. Stop whatever you are doing and take 3 deep breaths. Say a prayer in your heart for support and assistance from your inner voice. Remember to receive the support into your body by being in tune with your body's non-verbal, feeling sense.

2. Ask yourself, 'What in my life and the world is currently out of my control?' Make a list. Read the list one at a time and for each one add at the end, '… so I'm not going to worry about that today.'

3. What are you afraid won't happen for you (that you *want* to happen)? And what are you afraid might happen to you that you *don't* want to happen? Get these fears down on paper. Choose the top fear and put a number to it. Ask, 'on a scale of 1-10 how likely is this to actually happen/not happen?' Then ask yourself what actions you can take to help this thing happen (or not happen). Then either go and take those actions, or let go of worrying about it, knowing you have done all you can, and the rest is out of your control. Ask your inner voice or a higher power you believe in to take care of it.

4. Make a list of the things you are trying to create or accomplish in your life. Also make a list of your daily responsibilities. Now prioritize them. Decide which are important for right now and which can wait (or will *have* to wait so that you can maintain your sanity). Now plan for when you are going to work on your number-one top thing and how you are going to do that regularly.

5. Ask yourself whose voice is taking control over your unconscious mind right now. Is it a… parent, teacher, bully, Disney princess, priest, news anchor, politician, etc.? Imagine yourself standing in a blue-white cylinder of light with that person on the outside. Doing this will help separate your thoughts from theirs.

6. Answer these two questions: What feeling do I want to create? What accomplishments, events or relationships do I believe I need to have to attain them? Now, focus only on the feeling you want instead of the external things you think will create them. Next, offer that feeling to your inner voice. Ask for guidance on how to build a relationship with it and how to allow it into your life.

For building your pillar of creativity

1. Go out into nature and lay on the earth for as long as you can. 5 minutes, or 5 days. Simply allow your thoughts to be (though you may write them down in a journal if it helps). If your emotions are strong, allow them to overwhelm you. Cry, scream, stomp on the earth, whatever you need to do to free your heart.

2. Make a list of the negative things you fear might happen to you if people see you for who you really are. Then burn it.

3. Ask yourself, 'What events have recently transpired in my life that I'm afraid to feel? How have I recently chosen to be numb rather than express something important?'

4. Are you experiencing head chatter? Ask yourself, 'What am I unconsciously worrying about? How is the fear center in my brain hijacking my attention center right now and trying to get me to protect myself?' When you realize what you are worrying about, you can then find actions to take to protect yourself from what you are perceiving as dangerous. If you can't find actions you can take, ask for advice about it. There is always something. Even if you are not sure it will work, it's worth trying.

5. List 5-10 things you feel guilty about. Anything from your entire life. Sit in meditation with that list and ask your inner voice for guidance on how to move forward and never make these same mistakes again. Ask your inner voice how you can make it right and atone for what you have done.

6. Lay down and place one hand on your belly and one at the center of your chest. Take deep belly to heart breaths. Filling your belly all the way, then filling your chest, and then slowly exhaling. After a few cycles of breathing start to make a sound with your exhale. It can be a groaning, a roar, an 'ahhhhh'. Whatever comes to you. Do it as loud as you can. You can also move your arms and legs, shaking them or banging them on the floor or mattress as you release the sound.

7. Dance like a maniac. Take a mixed martial arts class. Do Cross-fit. Or otherwise move as much energy as you can through your body.

8. Stand in the center of a room and feel your feet sturdy on the floor. After a minute of standing take a stomping step forward and stretch your arms forward as if blocking somebody from approaching you. As you do this, say, 'NO.' Then step back into the center. Do this in each of the four directions. Keep going around in circles doing it until you naturally feel a desire to stop.

APPENDIX III: A DAILY INTUITION BUILDING AND MANIFESTATION PRACTICE

Whatever pillar you are currently building, the following exercise can help you. Especially if you do it regularly. Even if you only take ten minutes every morning and every evening for this, you will see remarkable changes in yourself in a very short time. If you do it three times a day, all the better.

Stepping into the circle.

1. Sit in silence and calm your breath for 1-5 minutes.

2. Invite whatever higher power or higher intelligence you believe in or simply call on your own inner voice to come and support you. Here you can do the Borderland Meditation if it helps.

3. State out loud the feelings and experiences you are grateful for. Really tune into those positive feelings you have experienced recently and offer gratitude for them. Focus on the feelings, not the external circumstances you think created them.

4. State out loud everything that you want and need in your life. Whether it's to help you build your inner experience of connection, receive a vision for yourself, ask for financial freedom, heal your relationships or more opportunities to share your gifts with the world. Anything and everything you need. The list can be long or short and it can be different each time you do this practice depending on what you need in that moment.

5. Imagine a white circle in front of you or actually draw one on the floor (or on a piece of wood you keep for this purpose). Stand up and step into the circle. If you are in public, you can imagine yourself doing this.

6. Inside the circle, imagine yourself under a waterfall. Standing with your palms facing forward and allowing the water to wash over you and then fill you. Stand in this way as long as you feel it is right for you. It could be 5 seconds or 5 minutes

or more. You can sit down if you want to. You can even lay down and completely sink into the experience.

7. When you are done, step back out of the circle and sit and integrate the energy you have received. The integration should be done by being aware of the sensations in your body - your *feeling sense*. Write down any ideas or images that come to you. Treat it like a brain storming session where self-censorship is not permitted. Simply allow what comes to you to come.

8. Finally, make a commitment to yourself to follow up on one of the ideas or images that came to you today and see where it leads you. No matter how small the action that you take, it is crucial not to skip this step. Without moving the energy through your body and out into the world, nothing will ever change.

9. Throughout your day, remember your white circle and imagine being filled up by the waterfall over and over again.

Note: It is ideal to focus on one big thing for a period of time, allowing that one thing to be your main focus. However, as things come up on a daily basis that you need support with, add them to the list after you name the main intention you are working with.

Optional: When you do this practice, use an object that is sacred to you and somehow represents what it is that you want in your life. Carry the object with you throughout the day to help you remember your intention and to make good choices for yourself. You can also leave it in a visible place in your house where you will see it regularly and sleep with it under your pillow.

APPENDIX IV: THE STREET CORNER PRACTICE

This practice is designed to help you practice tuning into your intuition so that when you are in the midst of an emotionally charged situation, you will feel trained and know what to do to center yourself. Just like military soldiers practice in warehouses built to look like the war torn area they are about to land in, you do this practice so that you instinctively know the moves you need to make to bring about positive outcomes in difficult situations.

The Street Corner Practice:
1. Find yourself a random street corner.
2. Do a short practice to connect to your inner voice and receive its sunshine from beyond the borderland.
3. Bring your vision to mind and ask your inner voice, 'which direction should I go in right now, this second, to further my vision?'
4. Receive the information from your inner voice and start walking.
5. Next street corner you arrive at, ask the same question.
6. As you walk, pay attention to your surroundings. See if your inner voice wants you to go into any stores or buildings.
7. If you get stuck and can't seem to get a clear direction to go in, focus on rebuilding your pillars. Ask yourself what you are afraid of or worried about. Ask yourself what 'I can't' voices are blocking you.

You can do this practice using any question or inquiry. For example: 'Which direction should I go in to make myself the happiest I can be today?' Don't do this practice while driving as part of the time you might be in an altered state.

APPENDIX V: DAILY PILLAR BUILDING PRACTICE

Set these reminders to repeat daily on your favorite calendar app. Personalize the experience by changing the words to your own.

Morning time - Vision

What is one thing I'm going to do today to move towards my vision?

Late morning - Connection

Am I experiencing any 'I can't' statements? Take a moment to connect to an internal source of love and nourishment.

Afternoon - Receptivity

Take a catnap, take a walk, meditate, sit under a tree. Get into the place in-between the moments and receive inspiration and support.

Evening - Creativity

Did I numb myself today? How can I express any pent-up emotions? What can I create tonight or tomorrow?

APPENDIX VI: SPINAL BREATH ALIGNMENT PRACTICE

The purpose of the practice is to help you release energetic knots that have built up in your body, especially in your spine and brain. There are two specifically recommended times to do this practice. First, as soon as you wake up in the morning, still lying in bed. And second, when you are going to sleep at night. That said, you can also do it anytime you are feeling stuck or out of balance.

The practice:

1. Ideally lay flat, but any comfortable position is fine.

2. Place one hand on your belly and one on your chest.

3. Start to breath fully and deeply, filling your belly first, and then your chest. Let the breath out slowly and completely. Notice if you start breathing solely into your belly or solely into your chest, as most people tend to gravitate to one or the other. If you notice yourself doing that, gently bring yourself back into full belly-to-heart breathing.

4. After breathing like this for a few moments start to visualize that with your in-breath you are pulling energy up through your feet. As the in-breath continues (filling your belly first and then your chest), the energy enters your spine and flows up into your brain. With the out-breath, the energy releases out the top of your head. Visualize the energy pouring out of you like a geyser or fountain.

5. Continue doing this circular breathing until you feel more balanced and aligned or you fall asleep.

Note: If you feel a specific place in your spine or anywhere in your body where there is tension, shift your practice to focus on that place. With the inhalation, breath the energy up from your feet into the tension. And with the out-breath, visualize it leaving through the crown of your head.

APPENDIX VII: FORGIVENESS RITUAL

Forgiveness is a crucial component of any spiritual work, especially for the work of clearing the heart of past pain. Forgiveness can't be forced, however - it's not something you can switch on or off at will. Forgiveness arises organically only when you experience compassion for another person, and when you learn to pull wisdom from your experiences. Wisdom that you can turn into action that makes the world a better place.

The Forgiveness Ritual:

1. Sit on your own in a safe place and think of at least one person who you still harbor resentment or anger towards. It can be something big or small - whatever you feel conformable with.

2. Put the name of the person down on a piece of paper.

3. Close your eyes, take a few deep breaths and ask your inner voice to show you that person's life and what led them to hurt you.

4. Do this until a natural desire to let go arises in you. Forgiveness can't be forced, it must happen naturally and organically through compassion.

5. When you feel the letting go happening, express any emotion that you have welling up from within you. You can do this by moving your body, writing, or making art. You can also express with voice and sound or simply call up a friend to talk and share.

6. When the self-expression is complete, ask yourself, 'What wisdom can I pull from having had this experience? What life lesson?'

7. Ask yourself, 'What action can I take to either heal this relationship or make the world (or my world) a better place as a result of my new wisdom?' This action might be to never have contact with the person again. It may be to reach out and ask for mediation or to approach them if you feel safe to talk. It may be that you are guided to something else entirely. Have faith in your inner voice no matter how odd its guidance seems.

8. Burn or bury the piece of paper with the name on it. This step is a very important part of letting go. Do not simply throw the paper away, and certainly do not keep it.

9. Write down your experience. If you choose to, share the results of the practice with a friend. There is nothing more powerful than being witnessed in your letting go.

You can also do this ritual as a self-forgiveness ritual. Instead of the other person's name on the page, put down your own. And then follow the same steps.

APPENDIX VIII: WHAT TO DO WHEN YOUR MIND SAYS 'I CAN'T'

Below is a list of 11 common 'I can't' statements that may pop up in resistance to being your authentic self. They are your unconscious self-sabotaging thoughts.

I want… But I can't because…

That's not how it is supposed to feel

When you have a specific expectation of what you are looking for (of what a desired experience is supposed to look like), you block the truth from coming forward. When you have a memory of how you experienced something at one time in the past, and you think it will be the same each time, you prevent yourself from receiving the most current and most medicinal version of what you are looking for. You prevent evolution and may feel bewildered, betrayed, frustrated or hopeless.

Suggestions: Invite yourself to become comfortable with the unknown. It is only from there that you will receive new perspectives. Invite your mind to become a blank slate. Open up to your inner voice and ask, 'show me where I'm not willing to accept the gifts that are being offered to me. Help me open to the new and unknown so that I can truly open my intuition.' Then sit silently and feel the answer in your body. First, as a non-verbal experience. Then wait for the answer to become images or words in your conscious mind.

That's not it, that couldn't possibly be the answer

Sometimes when you are looking for insight, you overlook it because it's not what you expect. When this form of resistance shows up it is because you believe the answer (or the feeling of what you are looking for) should be something other than what you are receiving or experiencing (even if unconsciously). Some part of you is unwilling or unable to see past your belief about it. You might feel confused, untrusting, bewildered, mystified or disbelief.

Suggestions: Be open to possibility. Suspend disbelief as if you are watching a TV show. Allow for the imaginary possibility of, 'This could be it… possibly… maybe…'

Even if you don't know what 'it' is and it's still just a feeling. Ask your inner voice for clarification on how this could be. Receive your answer in the feeling sense and let it soak into your body.

I don't want to change in this way

When you are particularly attached to a part of yourself, it is hard to let it go. Perhaps it protects you in some way. Perhaps at one point in your life it served a real purpose, or you are simply unable to perceive a 'self' without this component and that scares you. Maybe admitting this part needs to change means admitting that you held a strong belief about something for a long period of time that was wrong and it is hard to see that about yourself. You might feel afraid of change, annihilation or of seeing your own shortcomings.

Suggestions: Examine your unwillingness and the strength of your conviction. Do you really want a truthful answer to your query? Ask your inner voice: 'What habit am I attached to? What emotional pain am I numbing that I am unwilling to change? How can I strengthen my willingness to learn?' Ask to clearly and compassionately see the part of you that is still hiding. Let the answers come first in the feeling sense.

But I wanted/expected the answer to be…

You want the outcome to be something that you desire. A specific feeling or change in the world. But the answer that is coming to you challenges you to move beyond your desired outcome and into even greater possibility and maybe, you just can't see it yet. You might feel surprised, shocked, angry or betrayed.

Suggestions: Cultivate determination and the scientist's burning desire to explore, discover and uncover the truth. Be willing to adjust your hypothesis based on new information. You are being challenged to go beyond the known parameters of who you have been, and move into new territory. Ask your inner voice: 'How is my desired outcome holding me back from receiving new information from the unknown? Where does my desire for this particular outcome come from, and how is it keeping me stuck and preventing my growth?'

I can't do that / I'm not capable

To some degree, your inability to receive an answer in this scenario is because of a self-fulfilling prophecy. Notice if you felt depressed, incapable and helpless even before trying to move forward. It's a loop. If you feel incapable to start off with, you may unconsciously avoid getting an answer or getting what you want because it is exactly what you expect to happen. You might feel depressed, helpless, betrayed or weak.

Suggestions: In this scenario you will want to compassionately embrace your inner child. So, invite back your inner child's innocent excitement. Somebody or something taught that child that he/she was incapable. Maybe you were given the message that you couldn't accomplish certain things or unleash certain creative forces within yourself. Invite back what came before that. Find one small speck of that feeling of possibility, and gently put your attention on it. What you attend to, will grow.

Ask your inner voice: 'Did I ever believe that there was a way forward? If I did believe in a way forward, what would that feel like? If I were given unlimited support from sources that are currently unknown to me, would I feel capable?' Ask your inner voice for a feeling of possibility.

I don't know *how* that can be

In this scenario you ask a question of your inner voice and you get a feeling or an image of what the answer is, but you refuse to believe in that answer. You can't comprehend that you can do it, or that it could ever happen for you. Unconsciously, you dare not hope for it to be true! You might feel useless, despondent, confused, angry or frustrated.

Suggestions: When you are looking for answers, by very definition it means that you don't know how, and can't see a way. That is why you are doing this practice - to relax and receive the way forward from your inner voice. Embrace that there probably is a 'how' in existence that you currently can't see and are not consciously aware of at this time.

Simply wonder, 'Is there a path?' Don't try to define the path. Instead, look to your consciousness (into your feeling sense) for the feeling of the path that exists. Get the feeling of 'Yes' somewhere underneath the doubt, and feed it with your attention, gratitude, and deep mindful breathing. In a universe of infinite possibility, there is always a path to anything if you are willing to receive it.

It's too good to be true / I'm not worthy of it

You may be wondering if the happiness that you experience when you get the first real glimpse of possibility for yourself is going to be smacked out of you once you dare to experience it. It's like seeing the cookie jar and getting excited, but then having the fear of being disciplined, or of being denied your wish. This kind of scenario can happen over and over in a child's life and eventually, the child may start wondering if they even deserve goodness in life. You might feel shame, afraid to stand out, undeserving, or unable to contain happiness or blissful feelings.

Suggestions: Ask yourself for permission to rest. Ask to experience the feeling state of 'receiving that which I long for.' It might feel wrong to take something for yourself. But is it really? Just bring some doubt into that belief and ask to receive a new way. Try it and see if you get struck by lightning (even if you do, at least you will get struck by lightning while having the time of your life). If you still find yourself stuck on denying yourself that which is good, then you can promise to be of service to the world with your new-found freedom and abundance. That should create an opening.

I don't deserve it

It is a sad fact that so many of us have been given the message that we are to keep our heads and voices down lest they be beaten down. Shame, guilt, self-sabotage and self-ridicule have become part of almost every person's inner dialogue and culture. But no person needs to experience shame about who they are ever again.

Whatever your desires are, however you express creativity, and wherever your curiosity leads - in work, love, sexuality, or life, doesn't need to be held back. No matter how crazy you think it is, you deserve to experience it, to explore, to know and share your love in your own unique way. But if you are in resistance to that, you might feel unworthiness, guilt or shame over feeling good.

Suggestions: You deserve to be free. Accept the truth in this - that it is possible for you to receive love for simply being you. When you breathe this in, what does it feel like? Practice wearing this feeling for a while. Receive that reality for all of us - that everyone in the world is free to be the positive, creative human being that they are. Ask your inner voice: 'What if unleashing the full power of my creativity was welcomed, supported, desired and desperately needed by the world?' Enter the possibility of it. You probably offer this kind of permission to others, so why not to yourself?

But I've been bad!

Maybe you have abused your power in life. We all have at times. Maybe you have been oppressed by somebody who had power over you, so you identify power, resources and strength as bad. It's also possible that you have been fed a barrel of lies about yourself - that you have to be perfect or act a certain way in order to get rewards. Well guess what... It is completely untrue! You deserve goodness no matter who you are or what you have done. If you feel like you've 'been bad,' you might feel punished, jailed, shackled or stuck.

Suggestions: Out of all the others, this type of unconscious resistance may lead to the shedding of tears. Out of everything that we encounter in life, forgiving ourselves for our own misdeeds (even for other's misdeeds that we take responsibility for - we're crazy like that) is the hardest.

This 'I can't' statement is very often the objection that you will find at the bottom of the pit, underneath the rest, holding the glue of your unworthiness and sense of rejection together. But you can be your innocent self again! Invite this from your inner voice: 'What does it feel like to be my innocent self again? How am I blocking myself from receiving acceptance and success and why? How can I learn, grow and forgive myself?' What is the feeling of that?

That's not how I remember it.

You are looking for something that you are familiar with - some feeling from a previous experience. This makes sense - that experience was good and you want to duplicate it. But your experience of the world is ever evolving. Like a relationship with a lover. You have a honeymoon phase, and after that phase, you have to be willing to shift to something more sustainable. The first glimpse of inner peace is an epiphany. As you progress, it can look like many things, and point to many painful places that are in need of healing, so it won't always look the same. You might feel defiant, angry, confused, or feel a desire to be in control.

Suggestions: We are all addicted to the bliss of attaining a peak emotional moment. Yet, the simplicity of true connection is so much deeper. It's like floating in the cozy soup of eternity, living moment to moment in pure potential. See if you can get the feeling sense of that simple, juicy goodness. Ask your inner voice: 'How am I limiting myself with the familiar? Am I willing to let go of my peak moment so I can have a long-term relationship?' Be open to what your true experience is right now, in this moment.

There are external circumstances that are insurmountable.

'I don't have enough cash, enough time, enough knowledge, enough supporters…' What's most important to remember in this situation is that you only have a small fraction of the information about your current circumstances. You don't know who you are going to meet around the corner. You don't know what supporters will show up if you just let the world around you know the mission you are on. If you are not willing to see how your intuition is able to guide you to the external support that you need, you might feel lonely, abandoned, resentful or depressed.

Suggestions: Imagine you are walking a pathway in a maze to get to where you want to be and you can't see around the next corner. But when you get to that corner, all you need do is ask your inner voice, 'where do I need to go *right now* to get to where I want to be?' When you ask that question with an emphasis on 'right now,' you will always receive guidance. It might be to get a cup of tea and take a break. It might be to get on a plane to Korea. Trust your inner voice like you are an investigator following clues, never really knowing where they are going to lead.

If you learn to identify some of these fundamental reasons for resistance, you will be able to apply similar principles to melting away other objections. There are infinite variations of them, and yet they all pretty much consist of, 'I can't, because…'. Once you start identifying them and how they affect your body and breath, they will all come tumbling down like a house of cards. Freedom is found in a direct connection to your inner voice - just beyond your internal resistance to who you are. Receive your freedom! You deserve it!

Appendix IX: Why Use Guided Meditations?

The key to making deep systemic change in your mental and emotional conditioning is to enter into your non-verbal mind and make changes to it directly. Not doing so is what keeps you going around and around in circles - having insights into your deeper nature but never quite embodying that insight fully.

So how do you make systemic changes in your unconscious mind?

There are 5 ways of doing this.

1. Having direct, intense, experiences in your life such as chronic or life-threatening illness or a near-fatal accident. Something in your life that shocks you into a deep understanding of yourself.

2. A direct intervention from Grace. Yes, sometimes this happens. You get tapped by The Mystic and are transformed.

3. Plant medicines. Tools such as peyote that are used by Native Americans for spiritual awakening and healing.

4. Elongated periods of solitude and meditation. These periods lead your mind to tranquility and organically allow you to enter into the deep symbolic places inside yourself from a place of silence and connection to nature.

5. Initiation rituals. These rituals are what have been used for thousands of years in the inner circles of mystery schools, priest schools and monasteries to instill a direct experience of The Mystic in the recipient.

It is this last tool that the guided meditations created for Awakening to the Mystic were created to emulate. In fact, the guided meditations are more like Guided Initiation Journeys. In the ancient world, the spiritual practitioners of the time knew that people only experience real transformation through images and physical experiences. That's why they had elaborate rituals and elaborate initiation processes.

Additionally, the performers in these initiation rituals had the knowledge of sacred geometry, the movement of energy, archetype, and direct mystical revelation. So the practitioners who performed the initiations would call forward (invoke) those energies and embody them, symbolically acting as archetypal forces that the initiate encounters.

A guided initiation journey is not a simple guided relaxation exercise or guided meditation. It is a powerful symbolic journey that acts as an initiation ritual for your unconscious mind. An initiation is like the igniting of a fire, the turning on of a switch, or the planting of a seed which then grows into embodied transformation.

The guided initiation journeys of Awakening to the Mystic (A 40 day program created by Aaran Solh) allow you to gain new perspectives on your emotional and mental processes in a specific, strategic and focused way. Just like the ancient mystery schools did and just as modern ones continue to do.

Doing a specially designed guided initiation mediation (for emotional transformation or spiritual awakening for example) after reading about it is like reading about jogging and then going for a jog. Or reading about India and going to India. The one might prepare you for the later but you will never really know what something is like until you've had the direct experience! To make real change, you have to engage your senses, your non-verbal experiential nature, and your archetypal nature. In other words, your entire self.

The meditations created for Awakening to the Mystic are for people who want to do just that but don't want to go live in a cave. They are for people who want to take a deep dive into their symbolic, non-verbal mind without taking hallucinogenics. They are for people who understand (and on some level long for) the importance of ritual and ceremony but have no idea where to get it in this modern day of watered down religion.

The Awakening to the Mystic guided initiation journeys are symbolic journeys that, like the ancient initiation rituals, speak directly to the unconscious mind, bridging the gap between the intellectual and the experiential. You need to bridge the gap between those two parts of your mind if you are going to create real transformation in your life.

Learn more at www.AaranSolh.com

ACKNOWLEDGMENTS

To the thousands of people who trusted me to support them on their journeys of personal growth - thank you! Without you, I never would have had the ability to explore and appreciate the realm of intuition and how empaths and spiritual seekers struggle to connect with it. I also want to thank *you,* my reader, for being on the same dedicated path of connecting to your intuition and expressing your inner voice. The more you connect, the more you support a nourishing and compassionate world and a restoration of balance and harmony, so thank you for being part of that movement!

A deep and humble thank you to the early adopters of Awakening to the Mystic and to those who read the progressing versions of my book and provided invaluable editing and feedback: My genius wife Aryana, Jonathan Houghton, Helen Jordan, Jessica Huff, Erik Sterns, Navneet Kang, Hana Hoffman, Janice Hamilton, Janie Lawson, and Ilona Goossens. I couldn't have done it without you!

ABOUT THE AUTHOR AARAN SOLH

Aaran began awakening as an empath and intuitive at age 15. His spontaneous awakening started him on a journey of spiritual exploration that has spanned 3 decades and 5 continents. Along the way, Aaran apprenticed with healers, spiritual teachers, and shamans from a variety of traditions.

His apprenticeship studies and trainings include: Soul Retrieval, Shamanic Journeying, Conscious Dreaming, Rebirthing Breathwork, Rei-Ki, Cranio-Sacral Therapy, Energy Healing, Aromatherapy, Thai Massage, Psychic Development, Vortex Healing, Deeksha, Guided Meditation Facilitation, Bach Flower Remedies, and a variety of meditation techniques.

Aaran has also attended innumerable workshops, conferences, and retreats with modern spiritual teachers such as Adyashanti, John Perkins, Sandra Ingerman, Tenzin Wangyal Rinpoche, Gangaji, Brian Weiss, Deepak Chopra, and Pema Chodron. Aaran has also been a student of The Western Mystery Traditions (Kabbalah, Gnosticism and The Egyptian Mysteries) through the initiatory system of The Sodalitas Rosae Crucis & Sodalities Solis Alati since 2002.

In addition to his spiritual studies, Aaran graduated from The Evergreen State College with a Bachelor's Degree with an emphasis in Multicultural Counseling. He also studied Chemical Dependency Counseling and received training in Suicide Prevention and Teen Mentoring.

Aaran is also the creator of The Intuition Quiz and Awakening to the Mystic: A Roadmap for Empaths and Spiritual Seekers, a system of spiritual development based on universal mystical principles. He currently lives in the Pacific Island nation of Vanuatu with his wife and daughter where he enjoys teaching, coaching, eating lots of fresh fruit, meditating in nature, walking through the jungle, and splashing around in the ocean.

Please visit Aaran's website to learn about personalized coaching programs:
www.AaranSolh.com/About

Made in the USA
San Bernardino, CA
19 January 2020